TUR

ENDORSEMENTS

If you want to think differently about how to strengthen, grow and foster a healthy marriage, this book is for you. I would encourage couples to read it with an open heart and open mind. If you are not growing together, you will grow apart. Make the investment into your marriage with Turn It Up! Your relationship will be far richer for it. All In!

Dan Reeve
Lead Pastor
Faith Church
go2faith.com

Pastor Kelly DuPée is a gift to the body of Christ, his community, and our world! I have known Pastor Kelly for over 20 years and have the utmost respect for his commitment to others and the ministry he exhibits to those he serves. His book, Turn It Up! is a great example of his wisdom, which is dispensed in a way that can be utilized in practical relational applications. I highly recommend Turn It Up! to you, as you will find the needed ingredients you can apply in your own marriage, as well as other relationships, which will bring added value and blessing in your world.

Keith Hershey
Founder/President
Mutual Faith Ministries

Kelly DuPée has written a book important to any man or woman seeking a quality marriage. Whether you are about to embark on that great adventure called marriage, or are a "seasoned pro," Kelly's book has something for you. Kelly's personal examples and vulnerability lend an air of great authenticity, and his precepts are solid and well grounded. Easy to read and begging for the highlighter to mark significant passages, Turn It Up! is a gift you can give to yourself or someone you care about. I highly recommend it.

Dana Buck
Director of Engagement Programs
World Vision US (Retired)
Author of Sew Powerful Parables: Stories
of Rhyme, Reason and God's Truth

Many of the problems in today's society are directly related to the deterioration of the family unit. 40% of family formations today are single parents, usually women raising multiple children. Kelly's book is an easy read, it is direct and very targeted towards the primary reasons that marriages fail. Read it, have your spouse read it, then candidly discuss it together. You will be surprised with the results.

Richard Koon
VP Ministry Lending
America's Christian Credit Union

When I read this book, it was refreshingly different. It is a blend of Pastor Kelly's vast personal experience and sound research but features easy to understand questions at the end of each chapter designed to spark relevant conversations between the couple. I would recommend this book to anyone who is ready to take their relationship to the next level!

Nancy P Zybala, LMFT
New Dawn Head of Service

During my senior year of high school, I met the love of my life – my 1970 Mercury Cougar XR7 Hatchback with a roar that only a 351 cubic inch, 8-cyclinder V8 engine can produce. She was a real beau, with her bright blue metallic body, pinstripe hood and white hardtop, I was the envy of all the guys in the neighborhood. But over time, our relationship grew strained. I became burdened with many of life's distractions that slowly, and unnoticeably and unintentionally began to eat away at my sweet little deuce. Within a few years, I had to release her to the junk yard for spare cash that I desperately needed – all $200 worth.

Pastor Kelly is a friend of mine that I have trusted for many years. His wise counsel and deep compassion for people comes through in this book. This book will become part of my toolkit for maintaining and revving up my own marriage. Whether the occasional tune-up or a complete overhaul, this book is the perfect manual for maintaining that hum with your special someone.

John S. Miramontes
Architect

Pastor Kelly's Book Turn It Up! is a how to guide to achieving a lasting happy and successful marriage or relationship. Whether you need to improve a troubled marriage or want to maintain an already great relationship, Turn It Up! is a no-nonsense guide guaranteed to lead you to making positive changes in marriages and relationships. With faith in God as a foundation, Pastor Kelly emphasizes the importance of building and strengthening a good connection with your spouse or significant other and prescribes five easy to understand and effective steps on making positive and lasting effects to any marriage.

As a 25-year law enforcement veteran, this book has helped me identify some simple but important steps that I can take to maintain my own marriage. From an officer-wellness perspective, this book is a must-read for all of law enforcement; a profession plagued with a high divorce and suicide rate. There is no doubt in my mind this guide can make a positive change in all marriages!

Lt. Tony Cortina
West Covina Police Department
West Covina California

When I read Turn It Up! by Kelly DuPée my intentional love and behavior toward my beautiful incredible wife of 42 years increased and our relationship improved.

Pages 10 and 11 provided enough positive information and wisdom to make the purchase worthwhile for an opportunity to dial up the love in a good relationship, and perhaps save a struggling marriage. I cannot thank you enough Kelly, for this timely much needed book.

Rev. Andy Bales
President and CEO
Union Rescue Mission in Los Angeles

Every married person starts out with great intentions for their marriage. And as Kelly points out in Turn It Up! over time the dimmer switch of good intentions can be turned down. I believe the tools and skills Kelly provides in this book are not only practical but also necessary for having a lasting and successful relationship. If you need a tune up or just tools to stay connected, I highly recommend you read Turn It Up!

Steve DeYoung
Founding Pastor of Mountainview Church
Rancho Cucamonga, California

We have been getting coached by Pastor Kelly, and he has been able to coach us through our weaknesses and has helped us build on our strengths. The book has even elevated our relationship to an even higher level. The book is filled with real life challenges, and a variety of different ways to work on those challenges as a couple. If you want to turn up your marriage or relationship, this book will give you real useable tools that can help make a better, stronger, and closer connection with the love of your life.

Steve and Maria Orozco

Turn It Up! by Kelly DuPée is a powerful resource for married or soon to be married couples. Although it may be most impactful for newly married couples or those couples facing difficult times, the insights laid out here can be greatly beneficial to all married couples. Turn It Up! provides a practical, proactive plan that is easy to follow with a focus on strengthening marriage connections.

The five commitments and five skills Pastor Kelly has presented here cover all the bases of a healthy and blessed marriage while dealing head-on with the difficult issues many couples face. After reading Turn It Up! I was able to see some things in a different light that I was missing and have a guide that my wife and I can utilize to continue to build a great relationship that is blessed by God. I cannot wait to put into practice the commitments and skills in Turn It Up! that will get the dimmer switch in my marriage turned up to the highest setting and see my connection to my wife strengthen! Thank you, Pastor Kelly!

Matt Fitzgerald

In a time and generation where the world is competing for your every focus, Pastor Kelly DuPée reminds us of the importance to pay-attention to your connection, in our relationships and especially our marriages. He motivates you to understand that no relationship or marriage just magically succeeds or even fails, but requires each of us, to go to the dimmer switch, and Turn It Up!

Pastor Kelly DuPée's ministry and wisdom is like walking through an aisle of a library. He has impacted the lives and stories of thousands, including my own. Turn It Up! will challenge, inspire, and encourage your marriage to shine resplendently the way it was always meant to. I highly recommend this book if you are desiring to develop a stronger connection with your spouse!

Marriage is not a toggle switch; it is a dimmer switch. It is time to make your marriage shine!

Lead Pastor
Michael Alfaro
www.TheCallingla.com

Pastor Kelly will give you the practical tools and concepts to 'turn up' your relationship for a long, healthy, and meaningful marriage.

Jeff Mosley
Police Officer

Pastor Kelly has had, and continues to have, a huge impact on my life. I have had the pleasure to serve under his pastoral leadership at Faith Church and have grown in many ways through these years. He is a deep well of knowledge and wisdom which I am blessed to have drawn from. He has provided me guidance through difficult times in my life, helped me develop my leadership abilities, supported me in all areas of my life, and most of all, been an example of how to love God and love people.

I am currently engaged to be married soon and my fiancée and I admire the marriage that Pastor Kelly and Carrie have. In fact, Pastor Kelly will be officiating our wedding! This book is just a piece of what we see and experience from their marriage and through this book, they continue to have an impact on our relationship and our lives. My hope is that through this book you are also able to experience the love and care that Pastor Kelly has for you.

Elvis Chen

Kelly DuPée's book is a wonderful practical guide to having a strong and lasting marriage. His book reveals key areas and key commitments that couples need to make and practice every day in their marriage. As a Marriage and Family Therapist, I found the skills mentioned in this book very pertinent to having a healthy, loving marriage. The skill building section of the book can help couples before they even get married. Kelly gives the reader a how-to understanding with five skills that makes it easy to implement. The personal and professional stories give the book a broader understanding of what it takes to make a marriage connect.

Kelly DuPée's book is a wonderful practical guide to having a strong and lasting marriage. His book reveals key areas and key commitments that couples need to make and practice every day in their marriage. As a Marriage and Family Therapist, I found the skills mentioned in this book very pertinent to having a healthy, loving marriage. The skill building section of the book can help couples before they even get married. Kelly gives the reader a how-to understanding with five skills that makes it easy to implement. The personal and professional stories give the book a broader understanding of what it takes to make a marriage connect. The spiritual aspect of the book also provides a deeper understanding of how God designed marriage. Kelly's book is encouraging and motivating to read. I would recommend this to my family, friends, and clients.

MaryLou McGuirk, LMFT
Licensed Marriage and Family Therapist

If you value a strong and stable marriage, if you can still see that twinkle in your partners eye or if the flame in your marriage is trending low and you are wondering what to do, Turn It Up! is a must-read book for you. My name is Richard Bell and I have been married for over 31 years. I have a very noble job as the Police Chief of a mid-size Police Department. I have a wonderful family and from all accounts we are living a good life, full of blessings. I would say the strongest part of the family is my marriage.

I started reading Pastor Kelly's book and I could not put it down. As I read through it, I could not help but test some of the techniques against my own marriage. What I found was that no matter how strong you think your marriage is, it can always use a little "turn up." Sometimes we take for granted the little things in our marriage which often times turns into big things. The concepts presented in this book are relevant to today's marriages and extremely helpful if taken seriously. I was captivated by the very first chapter with the question "How is our connection." When I asked that question to my wife, I did not get the response that I expected. Although the overall answer was not bad, I realized a "turn up" was in order. The manuscript is thought provoking and challenges you as a person to pursue the best possible connection with your wife or husband. I know God honors the marriage union. Pastor Kelly is an experienced Pastor and Life Coach in the field of marriage. He adds insight and revelation in a controlled environment to help facilitate a healthy marriage.

Richard Bell
Chief of Police
City of West Covina

Kelly DuPée has written a practical guide to marriage that every couple should read. He openly shares about his own marriage and brings in the advice of many experts. He hits all the bases.

Bill Stephens

Why wait until there is no more time to save your marriage? Small daily but radical practices can build your relationship even stronger through the toughest of times.

A few years ago, my wife Ivonne was at the brink of death after being diagnosed with a liver and kidney chronic failure condition. Her health deteriorated faster than we could adjust. I was unsensitive, unresponsive, and even inappropriate at times. My clueless attitude did not help my wife much but was adding pain to her sorrow and suffering. Pastor Kelly stepped right in. He was fearless. He told me a couple of good and valuable truths that help me see my wife's needs clearly to respond accordingly. Then he turned to her and helped her navigate her uncertainty, depression, and anxiety. His advice helped us turn to each other with love and care. Together, we were able to tackle her health issue head on until she received a double organ transplant and recovered. Now she is in good health, but our marriage came out on top, in better health than we dreamt of. Thank you, Pastor Kelly, for your coaching guidance now condensed in this book.

Then…

Why wait to read Turn It Up! to save your marriage? Rush to come together starting today.

Vladimir Lugo
President & CEO
Tepui Cloud
https://tepui.cloud

TURN IT UP!

HOW TO HAVE THE LIFELONG MARRIAGE
THAT YOU REALLY WANT

By Kelly DuPée

Portable *inspira*

TURN IT UP!
HOW TO HAVE THE LIFELONG MARRIAGE
THAT YOU REALLY WANT
© 2021, Kelly DuPée

Scriptures taken from the Holy Bible, New International Version®, NIV®. Copyright © 1973, 1978, 1984, 2011 by Biblica, Inc.™ Used by permission of Zondervan. All rights reserved worldwide. www.zondervan.com The "NIV" and "New International Version" are trademarks registered in the United States Patent and Trademark Office by Biblica, Inc.™

©First Edition 2021 Portable Publishing Group LLC.
30 N Gould St, Ste R, Sheridan, WY 82801,
United States of America.

www.editorialportable.com

Portable Publishing Group LLC is a globally minded publisher supporting the work of independent authors. We believe in editorial diversity and new creators. Our digital and printed editions, which cover the most diverse genres, are possible thanks to the alliance between authors and publishers, in order to create books that cross borders and find readers.

ISBN: 978-1-953540-56-0

Printed in the United States of America

TABLE OF CONTENTS

To my loving wife Carrie. I love you now more than ever and dedicate this book to you. Thank you for your love, encouragement, patience, support and for abandoning the option to quit. You're the best and I'm still falling!

TURN IT UP!
FOREWORD

What is the first thing you look for when choosing a book to read? Or, perhaps, a movie you'd like to see or a television series to watch? Of course the subject matter is important – what is it about? If it's a Dodgers or Lakers game, or a major golf tournament, I'm in, no questions asked. If it is a movie I need a little more information. Is it an action flick, mystery, drama or a romcom? Are the reviews any good? But when it comes to anything informational and instructional I not only want to know *what* it is about I want to know *who* is coming up with the material.

They say *you teach what you know but you reproduce who you are*. Sure, there are successful coaches who were not outstanding at the game as players but have proven excellent at leading championship teams. Still, if you are going to help me live my life better you'll have to forgive me if I am very interested in how you are living your life – especially in regards to the topic you are teaching. This is nowhere more true than in the critical area of marriage.

Marguerite and I have been married for 49 years, so if for no other reason than longevity we have learned a thing or two about what it takes to succeed. We are going for the gold! For most of these years we have known Kelly DuPée. Over the decades I have ministered with Kelly, worked with Kelly, traveled with Kelly, played golf with Kelly, and can honestly say he is one of the finest men I've had the privilege to know. Of course he's not perfect, but when I think of a man of integrity he is one of the first that comes to mind.

I had the honor of performing the ceremony when Kelly married Carrie. Marguerite and I have both observed and lived life with them as they have grown from newlyweds to parents to grandparents. We have seen first hand their ups and downs and how they have handled multiple challenges and tackled various problems. Through it all I can safely say they have learned to *Turn It Up!*

Kelly writes in a straightforward, easy to understand manner, with numerous applications that benefit the reader immediately. While the book can certainly be utilized as a manual to heal and improve anyone's marriage, it does not read laboriously like a typical textbook. You will discover solutions for your life and marriage that have been hiding in plain sight.

Success in anything, including marriage, rarely if ever just happens. It happens by design, not default. One of my favorite Bible verses is Ecclesiastes 10:10, *"If the ax is dull and its edge unsharpened, more strength is needed, but skill will bring success"* (NIV). In short, you are never wasting your time sharpening the ax. Reading and even studying *Turn It Up!* will prove to be not so much an expenditure of your time and energy as an investment.

Sound like too much work? Well, if you're like me getting started is hard, but not as hard as you might think. In contrast, going through a divorce is always significantly harder and more costly than initially imagined. The long-term costs of deciding to simply check out through excessive partying, drinking, and drug use are enormous. No matter what you decide to do and wherever you decide to go there are costs. Even if in the end your marriage cannot be saved you will find yourself a better person by making wise choices now. Whatever happens in your journey you will not regret learning to ***Turn It Up!***

As you put in the work to better your life and marriage I encourage you to move beyond your feelings. It is common for a spouse to feel like they don't love their partner any more (they may even wonder if they ever really did love them). If that's the case, why try? I seldom feel like exercising and stretching but I do it about five times a week. Why? I don't like to exercise! But I do want to stay as strong and flexible as I can for as long as I possibly can. Also, I like the way it makes me feel (alright, only when I'm done!). If I waited until I felt like it I would seldom exercise. My friends in recovery have taught me a life changing truth – *it's easier to act your way into a feeling than to feel your way into an action.* For them, it is a matter of continued sobriety. For me, it is a matter of staying in shape as I age. For you, it might be a matter of reigniting a lost love and passion.

Maybe the willingness to put in the work is not your problem but the idea of having someone coach you is. I know that feeling. I tend to prefer jumping right in and figuring things out for myself. Taking the time to sharpen the ax or being coached seems unnecessary or overly time consuming. But I have learned that all too often what I feel isn't real. It took me a while to realize that what I thought I was doing in my golf swing was not what I was actually doing. It took an outside pair of eyes (and video!) to prove it to me. In fact in more ways than one what I felt I was doing was the exact opposite of what I was actually doing! My golf game improved exponentially when I allowed myself to be coached by quality people. Life and marriage are no different and way more important than golf. To work hard at what you feel is correct only to find out it is not right is disheartening, but that realization is a necessary step toward authentic improvement. For that to happen, we need help. And, by the way, Kelly is an insightful, proven and effective coach!

Marguerite and I are praying that as you journey through the book God will give you a breakthrough. ***Turn It Up!*** can help bad marriages become good and good marriages become great. But, as Kelly points out, the focus is on progress not perfection. *"I pray with great faith for you, because I'm fully convinced that the One who began this gracious work in you will faithfully continue the process of maturing you until the unveiling of our Lord Jesus Christ!"* (Philippians 1:6, TPT).

Dr. Jim Reeve

Founding and Senior Pastor
Faith Church, West Covina

Turn it up!

INTRODUCTION

WHY YOU NEED TO READ THIS BOOK!

Did you know there are two types of light switches? One is called a toggle switch. You flip it up and the light goes on; you flip it the opposite way and the light goes off. There is also a dimmer switch, which has a knob that you can turn up or down depending on the brightness of light you want.

What does this have to do with marriage or relationships? I like to think that there is an imaginary dimmer switch that controls the strength, health or quality of your marriage. If you want more light in your house, you can turn the real dimmer switch up. Likewise, if you want the room to be darker, a dimmer allows you to gradually adjust the light to what you would like it to be. A lot of people tend to think of the health or quality of their relationship as a toggle switch that is either on or off. You are either married or you are not; and, if you are married, it's either good or bad. The truth is, however, that a dimmer switch is a much better way to think about your marriage.

When you get married, you are excited about it and very much in love. During this time, you could say that your switch is turned all the way up. As time goes on and the challenges of life hit you, the brightness or quality of your relationship can start to dim as if someone turned it down. When you get busy, or spend a lot of time at work, or focus your attention on your kids, you gradually start drifting apart. What was once turned all the way up has now been gradually turned down. What was once dynamic and exciting has morphed into something routine and dull. However, just as life can turn the quality of a marriage down, you have the power to reverse that and to turn it up.

In a romantic relationship or marriage, everybody wants two things: for the relationship to be great and for it to last. The problem is that often we do not know how to get these things. How do you build a fulfilling and long lasting marriage with another human being? We all look at couples in their golden years that have been married for decades, thinking they either must be really lucky or really blessed. Certainly, there are some who have figured out how to be happily married. However, the sad reality is that most marriages or romantic relationships either end painfully or stay together while being unhappy. This does not have to happen to you. I have got good news: you really can have a great marriage that is enjoyable and fulfilling, AND that will last a lifetime. But this does not happen by accident. You have to intentionally turn it up.

This book will teach you how to have a long lasting and enjoyable marriage. I will show you how to monitor and turn up the heat in your connection so that you can respond and fix problems while they are still small. I will give you practical and easy-to-follow instructions on how to strengthen and sustain your marriage so that it will last a lifetime.

Before I tell you how to turn it up, let me tell you a bit about me and why you should trust that I know what I am talking about.

I have been extremely blessed in my marriage to the love of my life, Carrie, for over thirty years. We have had some challenges, as all marriages do; but we have overcome them, grown in our love and learned a few things along the way. I have the incredible blessing of serving as one of the pastors at Faith Church in the Los Angeles area and as a Chaplain for the West Covina Police Department. I am also a certified Life Coach that specializes in marriage coaching. In those roles, I have officiated hundreds of weddings, and have talked and prayed with hundreds of couples at different stages in their marriages. Some of them have been engaged and have come to me for premarital counseling. Some have been married and in need of input on specific issues. A few have come hoping that a conversation with me would keep them from filing for divorce. I have also taught and led marriage classes and programs. I am not a marriage counselor, a therapist or a psychologist; however, my own marriage, along with my experience helping couples, has given me some insights on how to make a marriage work.

I am passionate about helping you have and maintain a great marriage. I have seen too many divorces that could have been prevented. In addition to helping couples stay married, I have also helped individuals to recover from divorce and I have seen firsthand the devastation that is caused when a marriage dies. Although I love helping people in any way I can, I would always prefer to be at the top of the cliff, warning you to turn around, rather than waiting with an ambulance at the bottom to help after you have crashed.

So, what will you get from reading this book? Here are just some of the benefits. You will see why it is important to regularly check on the quality of your connection and to turn it up. You will learn things that you can consistently do to turn up the passion, love and fulfillment within your marriage.

You will learn how to protect your connection from outside influences that could turn it down. You will learn how to ask for what you need. You will learn how to solve problems together, avoid conflicts and deal with the challenges that inevitably arise along the way, that can also turn down the strength of your connection. You will learn how to deal with negative emotions, like anger, in a healthy way so that it will not damage your relationship. In short, you will learn how to turn up the strength of your connection, which will result in you having a great marriage.

This book contains wisdom that I have gleaned from many other sources that have poured into our lives, such as Dr. Jim and Marguerite Reeve, the senior pastors at Faith Church who have been married for almost fifty years. Their wisdom and example have been an inspiration for thousands of people, including us, and we are very thankful for that. I have also taken some of the best ideas from other experts in marriage and relationships, and condensed them into the easy-to-follow concepts that you will find here.

This is a how-to kind of book, a manual to follow so you can learn how to be married. The instructions and suggestions I make are time tested, and many of these concepts have been proven by research done to help couples have a stronger and better relationship. Let me assure you that these are things that Carrie and I have applied and continue to practice on a regular basis; not just theories that I think would work. They have been tested, evaluated and applied to real life relationship challenges, and are proven to work.

Here is my promise to you. If you read and apply the concepts in this book, your marriage or relationship will improve and become stronger. I cannot promise that it will last a lifetime: this is up to you and your spouse. But I do promise that the stronger the connection you have with your spouse, the better your marriage will be; and you will survive the storms and challenges. If you do not put into practice what you read in here, I can guarantee that you will not have the practical wisdom that could help you have a great and long lasting relationship.

Who is this book for? If you are just getting started in your marriage, this book is for you. If you have been married for a while, but have hit some bumps and realize you need help, this book is for you too.

I have heard that pain pills sell better than vitamins. Unfortunately, we seem to only look for help when we are hurting, instead of taking proactive steps to improve our health. This book will not help you unless you read it. Do not wait until your marriage or relationship is in trouble to do so. The time to repair the roof on your house is before it rains. If you wait to read this book, you will not only miss out on a better quality for your relationship, but you will also be unprepared for the storms that will hit it. Think again of what you want in your marriage. You want it to be great and to last. I believe this book will help you achieve both of those goals.

If I have not convinced you yet to read this book, let me give you one more reason: your children. If you have kids or want to have kids, what kind of marriage would they want you to have? Would they want parents who are always fighting, arguing or, worse yet, avoiding each other because of unresolved issues? Would they want you to separate from each other? Would they want you going to court to decide who gets to live with whom? No. They want to see you talking, enjoying each other and working through the challenges in a healthy way. They want to feel and know that they live in a secure family, so they can thrive and grow into healthy adults who will also know how to be married. You can give them all of these things.

This is a book based on reality. Recently, I was teaching this to a group of engaged couples, where I could tell that some of these concepts contradicted the romantic ideas they had about life and marriage. I could tell I was bursting their bubble. I was not trying to depress them by explaining how challenging being married can be, but to give them a clear idea of what they were stepping into. Many couples feel they do not need to learn how to be married, they just want to figure it out on their own. Perhaps, that is why so many marriages do not make it. That is not what I want for you: I want you to know the pitfalls that could destroy your marriage so you can avoid them. I also want you to know how to respond in a more effective way when conflict arises. The truth is that your marriage will face challenges, but you can overcome them and pass the tests when you are prepared.

So do not wait, get started now. Read, talk about and apply the concepts presented in each chapter. We will first talk about why the connection between the people in a marriage or relationship is so important and about how to monitor it. Then, I will give you five commitments you need to make and five skills you need to learn how to use with each other. A commitment is a promise, followed by action, that is lived out on a daily or regular basis. These commitments are ongoing behaviors that when you do them regularly you will keep life from turning your connection down —and instead turn it up. A skill, however, is a tool that you learn and then use when it is required by a certain situation. By living out the commitments and using the skills, you really can have the kind of marriage that you want. One that is enjoyable and fulfilling, AND that will last a lifetime.

Are you ready to turn it up? Then let's begin!

Turn it up!

PART ONE
CONNECTION

CHAPTER ONE

THE CONNECTION QUESTION
"How's our Connection?"

I will never forget the day when my wife Carrie said to me that she was not happy with our marriage. At that time, we had been married for five years or so, we had two kids and I thought everything was going great. I honestly do not remember the exact words she said, but she made it clear that she needed something from me that I was not giving her. She wanted me to do things that would make her feel loved. She wanted to feel she was special to me. I pointed at everything that I was doing around the house, and at how these actions sent the message that she and the kids were my priority. She told me that she was grateful for that, but she needed more. She gave me some suggestions like writing notes or giving inexpensive gifts to her, just because I loved her. She also craved my time; she wanted me to be home with her and the kids as much as I could because that also showed how much I loved her.

I went to bed that night and thought about how I could change. Her requests were not outrageous, they were reasonable. I realized that I needed to change on the inside and consciously thought about what I could do to make my wife feel special. The next morning, I got up early, went to buy fresh bagels at a shop in the neighborhood, made coffee, cut a rose from our garden, put it in a vase and brought her breakfast in bed. When she saw my response, she cried because she realized I understood her concerns. I responded in a way that demonstrated that I indeed loved her and that she was special to me. I am so thankful she had the courage to say something to me back then. We have been married now for over thirty years and, to this day, one of my top priorities in life is to make my wife feel special.

However, this conversation could have gone completely different. Suppose I had responded defensively and given excuses for the way I was treating Carrie, rather than listening to her concerns. Suppose I had started to blame her for the problem. I could have said, "It's your fault; if you were a better wife, I would be a better husband." Another way I could have responded is by listening, but then minimizing her concerns and simply keep on doing what I was doing. One more possible response could have been to reply with cold indifference, to let her know that I simply did not care about her concerns. If I had responded in any of these other ways, I wonder if our marriage would have lasted. The quality of it surely would have gradually diminished, and perhaps one day she would have blindsided me and asked for a divorce.

How divorces develop

As a pastor, marriage coach and chaplain, I have both couples and individuals come to me with marriages that are heading for divorce. The saddest part about the conversations I have with people in that situation is that many times it could have been prevented. Great marriages do not just happen, neither do divorces. Something occurs and I am suggesting to you that the first thing to go in a marriage is the connection between a husband and his wife. Many times it is not an adulterous affair which causes a divorce, but a simple drifting apart.[1] This happens when things turn down

Turn it up!

the health of a marriage and the couple does not know they can turn it back up.

Drifting apart is actually a betrayal. When a couple drifts apart, it is because one person is putting someone or something ahead of their spouse and marriage. This could be caused by spending time and developing a closeness with someone else instead of your wife or husband. It could also be prioritizing your work or hobbies over your marriage. Either way, your spouse will feel that they are not as important as something or someone else.

When a couple begins to drift apart and their connection weakens or someone in a relationship feels betrayed, one person notices it and usually says something. Women do tend to be a little more relationally attuned and sensitive to the quality of a connection. Because of that, it is often the wife who notices the drifting apart. She then goes to her husband and tries to talk to him about this, so that they can turn it up again. Often the husband does not see that anything is wrong, so he does not do anything about the situation. Her concerns are met with indifference and nothing changes. The relationship continues to weaken and she feels more lonely and isolated.

The one trying to connect can be called *the pursuer* and the one ignoring the pleas for connection can be called *the pursued*. Eventually, the pursuer gives up trying to connect and starts looking for love elsewhere. This is often where the extramarital affair or at least an emotional intimacy with another person comes into the picture.

Finally, the pursuer decides that she wants out and asks for a divorce. Her husband, the pursued, is completely blindsided. He was so oblivious to his wife's needs that he did not see this coming. Once he is forced to face the ending of the marriage, he then springs into action and tries to change. He then tries to be the husband that his wife wanted him to be and to reestablish their connection. But oftentimes, it is too little too late. It's the proverbial closing of the barn door after the horse has already run away and the marriage ends in divorce.

I am not saying that all divorces can be prevented, but I am suggesting that some can. The answer is to first look at the quality or brightness of your relationship, by asking the connection question regularly and then responding by turning it up again.

The connection question

The connection question is three or four simple words that will cause you to evaluate and hopefully energize you to do something to strengthen the quality of your marriage. The connection question is: "How's our connection?"

A connection between two people is a sense of closeness, the sense of safety and security you get when you have a strong bond with someone. You trust that person to not hurt you or leave you. You have fun and enjoy being with them. It does not matter what you do together, you enjoy the moment because they are with you.

Connections must be monitored

Asking the connection question is how you monitor its quality. When someone gets hurt and the ambulance arrives, they check the patient's vital signs. In the same way, couples who want to stay married look at and talk about the quality of their connection. Whether they verbalize it or not, they regularly ask, "How's our connection?" If they do not feel it is as strong as it could be, they turn it up.

There are several reasons why couples do not ask the connection question and, thus, do not monitor the quality of their connection. The first is ignorance. We do not know that we need to. We think that, once we have a connection with someone, it stays good until something bad happens that damages it. If you think of being connected as an off and on toggle switch, there is no reason to be concerned about it. Once it's on, it's on; and there is nothing you have to do unless something happens to turn it off. But as I said earlier, it's more like a dimmer switch that can be turned either up or down.

Another reason we do not ask the connection question with our spouse is overconfidence. This is the "if it isn't broke, do not fix it" mentality. Unless there is a problem, many people do not think they need to do anything about their marriage or relationship. It is only when something goes wrong that they notice that they are not as close as they used to be. We need to realize that marriages or relationships and connections tend to degrade over time, unless you turn it up.

The result of ignorance or overconfidence is a false sense of security. I am not suggesting that we all become paranoid and insecure about our relationships. I do not want you to be constantly asking yourself if your marriage is ok. What I am proposing is that you do not take your relationship or marriage for granted. When you do this, you assume that it will always be the same as it is now and that there is nothing that needs to be done to improve or maintain it. You also tend to value it less. Unfortunately, people in many marriages take it for granted and then, when a challenge hits, their marriage collapses and its weakness is revealed for all to see.

Asking the connection question is living in reality. We may think we have a stronger connection than we actually do. When you take the time to look at the strength of your connection, you are stepping out of the realms of denial and fantasy into the realm of reality. If you have a great connection, rejoice! If it needs work, do not be discouraged and do something to turn it up. Nothing will happen until you embrace the reality of your connection and honestly look at the quality of it.

There are several ways to ask the connection question. Here are some suggestions of other questions that you and your spouse can use as a starting point for conversations.

1. How are we doing as a couple?

2. Is there anything you want to see different or changed in our relationship?

3. What do you like about our marriage?

4. Is there something you would like to see more of in our marriage?

5. Is there something that you would like to see less of or stop that's occurring in our marriage?[2]

6. What adjustments can we make to improve our marriage?

7. Is there anything you would like to talk to me about?

8. Are you satisfied with the quality of our connection?

9. What ideas do you have about strengthening our marriage?

You do not need to cover all the questions in one sitting, but you can imagine how your relationship will improve by

Turn it up!

just taking a few minutes regularly to talk about the quality of it. Items can be brought up by either of you, little problems can be resolved before they become big ones and you can take proactive steps to strengthen your connection.

What do you want?

What do you really want your marriage to be like? Do you want one that is strong, healthy, vibrant, supportive, beneficial, encouraging and loving? If you are engaged, what images come to your mind when you think about being married? You are probably picturing a relationship that you enjoy. You are probably thinking about a marriage that is marked by mutual love, respect, trust, support and encouragement. No one wants a marriage that is full of conflict, arguments and strife. We all want our marriage to be a place that is safe emotionally. We want to look forward to coming home after a hard day at work, being greeted by someone who loves you and then spending time with that person. No one wants to have a marriage that fails. We all want a marriage that will make us happy. We all want a great marriage. If you want to have an average one like everyone else, just do what everyone else does. But if you want a great marriage, you need to do something more.

A great marriage is not one that is problem or conflict free. It is one where both spouses are committed to each other, love being with each other and know how to serve each other in a way the other person appreciates. A great marriage takes work because it starts with two messed up people who each have lots of problems and issues. A great marriage is one where grace and forgiveness are given to each other liberally. When challenges hit a great marriage, the couple is able to weather the storm because they trust each other and recognize that they can prayerfully problem solve together.

I believe that a great marriage is something everyone can have, but the key is to continually monitor the quality of your connection and then turn it up.

Three stages of marriage

There are three stages that all marriages experience: honeymoon, reality and transformation. At first, everything is wonderful in your relationship. Either there are no problems or they are so minimal that you do not even notice. You are in love and your feelings of love can sometimes blind you to situations. This is called the *honeymoon* stage and it usually lasts the first year or two of a marriage. The next phase is called the *reality* stage. This is where you learn your spouse is not perfect. They do things that annoy you and you start seeing the person you married for who they really are. The third stage is *transformation*. This is where both people in a marriage decide to make it work. You blend your strengths and compensate for each other's weaknesses. You accept each other for who you really are and overlook those things that annoy you. In other words, you form a connection. As you go through the *reality* stage of your marriage, monitoring the quality of your connection regularly will empower you to take the necessary steps to move into the *transformation* stage.

A strong connection produces a quality marriage

Turning up the quality of the connection you have with your spouse will also make your relationship a lot more fun. The closer you are to a person, the more enjoyable it is to be with them. You will get a lot more out of your relationship when you have a strong connection.

A quality connection also results in creating a lot more positive things about your relationship than negatives. When you think about your relationship you feel satisfied and thankful for the wonderful person that you are connected to. A wife could say to herself, "Yes, my husband has faults and isn't perfect, but I love and appreciate who he is; and I am thankful for the strong connection I have built with him."

You were created to connect

God created you to want and need connections with others. There is a reason you got married. And if you are engaged, there is a reason you want to get married. You want to form a connection with someone. You want to share your life with another person, loving and caring for them. You also want that person to love and care for you. We all want to love and be loved. God made you this way. God said, "It is not good for the man to be alone. I will make a helper suitable for him." (Genesis 2:18 NIV). God's plan is for each of us to do life with other people. You start out in life getting these connections from your family. Then you form friendships with others in the neighborhood or at school. Later, you fall in love with someone and want to be with that person for the rest of your life. God wants you to have good quality connections with others and he also wants to see your marriage succeed. He is with you and for you. He will give you the strength, creative ideas and wisdom to have a strong connection that will result in a great marriage.

Marrying your soul-mate does not mean you will have a strong connection

Some people think that only others that are special or blessed can enjoy a great marriage, or that it all comes down to finding the right person. Nothing could be further from the truth. I do not believe in the concept of a soul-mate. As I understand the way the term is used today, a soul-mate is the one person who is perfectly suited for you. Once you find them, you have it made in the shade! You will never fight or quarrel! When you marry your soul-mate, you will not have to work at your relationship or ever have to ask the connection question. However, marriage is the collision and blending of two people with different ideas, dreams, values, personalities, likes and dislikes. Marriage takes compromise, understanding and the willingness to yield your point of view and embrace that of your spouse. Marriage is challenging and takes effort, but it is worth it.

I do believe, as we surrender our lives to God, that he leads us and gives us his best. When I was single, I asked God to give me the best wife and I believe he did. Over the years, Carrie and I have invested a lot of time and energy into the quality of our connection. This investment has paid great dividends and I am more in love with her now than ever. Second only to sending his son to die on the cross for me, the greatest gift God has given me is my marriage to Carrie. She is loving, kind, beautiful -inside and out- and also wise. She is not perfect and neither am I. We are both flawed; broken human beings who need Jesus to save us. We are both in the process of growth and God is continuing his good work in each of us.

Maintaining your connection

Asking "How's our connection?" empowers you to ask another question: "What can we do to turn it up?" That's what the rest of this book is about. In the following chapters, you will learn how to turn it up by making the commitments and using the skills that I will teach you.

If you want your car to last, you have to do preventative maintenance. You take it to the mechanic, even though it is working fine, to have the oil changed; also, if needed, worn out parts like belts and brakes get replaced before they break. You have a choice, you can either take care of your car or you can get stuck on the side of the road when it stops working. The same is true in a relationship. You must maintain and strengthen the connection with the person you love. Not only does your connection need to be monitored, it needs to be strengthened in order to last. In other words, you have got to turn it up!

Conclusion

What do you want your marriage or relationship to be like? The quality of your connection will determine the quality and sustainability of your marriage. To have a great marriage that will last, you need to regularly ask, "How's our connection?" We fail to realize that the strength of our relationship will gradually diminish, just like a dimmer switch being turned down. If that connection is not strengthened, it will weaken and eventually cease to exist. But when you ask the connection question and do things to turn it up, your connection will thrive, your marriage will be more enjoyable and it will last a lifetime.

With each other:

1. What factors do you think cause the connection in a marriage to gradually diminish?

2. What stage of marriage are you in: honeymoon, reality or transformation?

3. Ask yourself "How's our connection?" and then talk about it with your spouse.

PART TWO

FIVE
COMMITMENTS
TO MAKE

CHAPTER TWO

COMMITMENT # 1

BECOME ONE WITH EACH OTHER

I commit to becoming one with you

On your wedding day, you made promises and vows. The words you spoke before your family and friends, your church and your God changed everything in your life. Many engaged couples focus more on the wedding day than they do on preparing to be ready for marriage. The wedding is just the beginning and every married person will tell you that *being* married is a lot harder than *getting* married. To have a great connection and a great marriage, you first need to know the goal or purpose of it. What do you think the purpose of marriage is? Is it just to have someone with whom to share your life? Have sex? Raise kids? What is being married all about? What is the goal of being married?

God's plan for marriage

To answer these questions, we need to see what God says about marriage since he created it. In Genesis, we read about the first marriage between two people named Adam and Eve. God created the world and all that was in it, then he created

Adam. God said that his creation was good, but later he saw something that was not. The LORD God said, "It is not good for the man to be alone. I will make a helper suitable for him." (Genesis 2:18 NIV). It was not good for the man to be alone, so God created Eve.

Remember that Adam was asleep when God did this. When he woke up, God presented Eve to him. Before all this took place, God had given Adam the task of naming all the animals. In doing so, Adam saw that there was not another being like him. That is why, when Adam first saw Eve, he said: "This is now bone of my bones and flesh of my flesh; she shall be called 'woman,' for she was taken out of man" (Genesis 2:23 NIV).

Adam saw that Eve was made not only from him, but also for him. She was a perfect match. God then tells us the purpose of marriage. "That is why a man leaves his father and mother and is united to his wife, and they become one flesh" (Genesis 2:24 NIV).

Five times in the Bible (Genesis 2:24, Matthew 19:4-6, Mark 10:6-9, 1 Corinthians 6:16 and Ephesians 5:31), God tells us that his plan for marriage is that two people become one. It must be important if God felt the need to say it over and over to us. Becoming one begins with the vows you make on your wedding day and it is demonstrated physically through the sexual union. As you and your spouse spend time sharing your hearts with each other, you are united emotionally.

Being married is all about two people becoming one for the rest of their lives, which is all about growing closer to each other, establishing and maintaining a strong connection. When a relationship begins, you really do not know each other very well; but as it progresses, you discover more about each other. You learn about your spouse's likes, dislikes, values and you see their personality in everyday situations. As you get to know each other, you feel closer and your connection forms. The goal of a marriage for the rest of your lives is to grow in your oneness, in other words, to consistently strengthen the connection you have with each other.

Think of your lives as two circles that overlap, just as in this diagram. The part that overlaps is what you have in common and your goal is to increase that. The more you do it, the closer you will be to each other, the stronger your connection will be and the more you will be one.

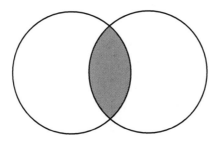

To turn up and strengthen your connection, you first need to commit to the process of becoming one with your spouse. Therefore, the first commitment we will talk about is: "I commit to becoming one with you".

Becoming one requires leaving home

Becoming one with each other starts by leaving home. The first part of Genesis 2:24, "a man leaves his father and mother", is critical. In order to unite to your spouse and start the process of becoming one, you first have to leave your father and mother. I will never forget a young couple that came to me a few months after their wedding. They had gotten into a fight and he had run home to his mother. This was a big mistake on his part for two reasons. First, the person he needed to talk to was his wife, not his mother; they needed to address the issue and work it out. The second reason why this was a mistake was that it damaged the relationship that his wife was trying to build with her mother-in-law. By the way, they worked through this and got back on track, and now they have been married for over ten years.

As a child, the most important people in your life are your parents. Unfortunately, many of us are raised with only one parent, often the mother. She may have become very significant in your life and that is a good thing when you are single. But when you are married, the most important person in your life needs to be your husband or wife. Leaving your parents does not mean to completely cut them off from your life or never talking to them again. It means the connection you are forming with your spouse will be strengthened when you create some space, both emotionally and physically, between you and your parents. So it is probably not a good idea to live with them in the same house, unless it is just a temporary situation.

Creating space means you no longer look primarily to your parents for comfort and encouragement. Instead, your wife or husband becomes your source of emotional strength and primary confidant. It is fine to go to your parents to ask for their input on financial matters or major decisions, but it is not healthy to let them dominate your life or relationship.

Parents must let go

This means it is wise for parents to stay out of things that are none of their business. They need to let their kids go. I have seen many parents hang onto their sons or daughters

Turn it up!

after they get married, which hinders the "becoming one" of the marriage and creates a dynamic that is not good for either relationship. If you have a parent that is hanging onto you just a little too much, you need to have a very straight and loving conversation with them. Let that parent know that, while you appreciate all they have done to help you grow into the person you have become, things need to change.

Just before I got married, I had a conversation with my mom and explained to her that things were going to be different between us afterwards. I told her that Carrie was going to be the most important woman in my life. She agreed and supported me in this, even though she was a widow and I was her only child. For 18 years, until she went home to heaven, my mom never interfered in our concerns. During our first year of marriage, knowing that Carrie and I needed time and space to bond, she moved to Texas to live with my aunt so that we could rent her house and get our marriage off to a good start. When she moved back to our area, we talked things over with her regularly, visited her weekly, and then later we bought a house where we could build a back house on our property so she could live with us.

If you have highly involved parents and are wondering how to have with them the kind of conversation that I had with my mom, here are a few suggestions.

1. Start with appreciation and acknowledgment. Let your parents know that you love them and appreciate all that they have done for you. If possible, think of specific ways your mom or dad supported and encouraged you and acknowledge that.

2. Address the fact that your life is changing because you are getting married, but that you want to stay connected to them. It will just be in a different way.

3. Clearly let them know that the most important person in your life will now be your spouse, but that you also are committed to staying connected to them.

4. Provide a specific plan on how you will remain connected while prioritizing your marriage. For example, you can say "we would like to come over for dinner once a week." Another possibility is to promise to call regularly to update them on what is new in your life. Letting them know how you plan on spending the holidays during your first year of marriage will also be helpful.

5. Give your parents time to respond. They may have questions, or they may just want to let you know how proud they are of you.

It starts with acceptance

Once you have "left" your parents, the next step in becoming one with your husband or wife will require you to accept him or her for who they really are. A very common mistake some people make is believing they can change the flaws of their significant other. If you think you can "fix" your spouse, this attitude will destroy your relationship and lead to a lot of frustration.

All of us have strengths and weaknesses, good traits and not so good ones. In order to create and sustain your connection with your spouse, it is critical to accept them "as is." The saying is true: "What you see is what you get." Yes, people can grow and change over time, but no one can change another person. If you notice a defect or pattern in your significant other before you get married, you need to ask yourself if you can live with that for the rest of your life. If you think not, then do not marry that person.

Love can be blind, so you may not see the potential problems that can arise because of differences in values, personalities or beliefs. This is especially true in matters of faith. We need to remember what God also tells us: "Do not be yoked together with unbelievers. For what do righteousness and wickedness have in common? Or what fellowship can light have with darkness?" (2 Corinthians 6:14 NIV). If you have fundamentally different values and beliefs than your spouse, you will probably not have a strong connection and you will struggle to grow closer, as your different values will constantly be in conflict. This verse, however, does not mean that you need to look for a spouse who is just like you. What is the fun or adventure in that? Opposites are often attracted to each other and able to balance each other out. This is the beauty of any close relationship: being able to expand and grow to become better together, better than we could ever be alone.

At some point, the same things that once attracted you to your spouse may start to annoy you. But remember: neither you, nor your spouse, is perfect. So ask God to give you grace and unconditional love so that you can accept your spouse for who they are. Becoming one is all about blending two people. Their struggles, issues, disabilities and defects are as much a part of the commitment as their strength, intelligence, differences and assets. Accepting each other fully and completely is absolutely foundational to have a strong connection and, thus, have a great marriage.

A great way to change how you perceive your husband or wife is by focusing on their good qualities, not just their negative ones. Thank God for your spouse and for the gift that they are to you. Instead of complaining or tearing them down with mean words, speak words of love and acceptance. Remind them of how much you love and appreciate them. This will change your heart and create an atmosphere that may give your spouse the courage that they need in order to grow.

If there are specific behaviors that your spouse does that are damaging to your relationship, those need to be addressed. Your spouse needs to know that you accept them unconditionally, and that you are *with them* and *for them* on the journey, no matter where it leads. In my ministry to alcoholics, I have learned that God wants his church to accept and love people who struggle with addictions unconditionally, just as He loves us. God's word tells us to: "Accept one another, then, just as Christ accepted you, in order to bring praise to God" (Romans 15:7 NIV). If you struggle with accepting your spouse, think about your own failures and inconsistencies. Realizing you are not perfect and also need acceptance will help you have grace with them. The key is to think about how Christ has accepted you with all of your weaknesses, flaws and struggles.

Your spouse will never grow or overcome their defects unless they know they are loved and accepted. Carrie was concerned a few years ago about my weight. She is a nurse and knows that I have a family history of heart disease; so she asked me the day after my birthday if I wanted to know what she wished for hers, which was in six months. I said: "Yes, I want to know what you want." She told me that she would like me to lose fifteen pounds. I immediately agreed and took it on as a challenge. I did not feel condemned, judged or rejected because Carrie accepts me for who I am and loves me unconditionally.

When you know you are loved, you can look at your faults and receive input from others without feeling rejected. Love and acceptance provide the safety that both you and your spouse need to grow and overcome challenges. Knowing you are accepted and loved allows you to establish and maintain

Turn it up!

a strong connection. When your husband or wife knows they are accepted, they can decide on their own to address a character weakness and draw on you for support. If they feel condemnation or rejection, they may never change. By the way, on Carrie's birthday I sent her a picture of me standing on a scale, showing that I had lost sixteen pounds!

Make decisions together

Once you leave home and accept each other, the way you become one starts with your attitude or mindset as you make decisions. Committing to becoming one with each other means that it is no longer about "me," but "we." Yes, you will have your own opinions, desires and needs, but you will make decisions as a couple. In a marriage, one person does not make all the decisions and just informs the other about what has been decided. No, it is about talking things over, sharing opinions and then deciding things together. The prophet Amos asks, "Do two walk together unless they have agreed to do so?" (Amos 3:3 NIV). Agreement does not mean you should see eye to eye on every issue; but it means you should talk it over and come to an agreement, or make a decision that both of you fully endorse. This is especially true when it comes to the major decisions about where you will live, what careers you will pursue, what jobs you will take and how you will raise your children.

Making decisions together increases wisdom. You and your spouse bring different perspectives to decision making. You bring different backgrounds and experiences. Rather than dismissing or minimizing your spouse's perspective or experience, welcome and listen to each other. In this way, you may prevent mistakes that could have devastating effects. This is especially true when it comes to finances, which I will discuss more in Chapter Eleven.

Win/win or win/lose

As you make decisions together, work on creating win/win arrangements. Unfortunately, some couples live in the world of win/lose. A win/lose situation occurs when one person gets what they want and the other feels like they have lost. This is usually okay with the loser once in a while. However, resentment will soon build when one person continues to lose in the decisions that are made. When resentment builds and builds, it eventually explodes into a full-scale fight with lots of pent up frustration, finally being released in a wave of hostility.

A second thing that can happen in a win/lose relationship is the resignation by the one who loses. He or she feels that they never get what they want; so what is the point of expressing their opinion? This person feels so undervalued that they stop trying to contribute. They resign themselves to a role as the subservient member of the marriage and emotionally check out. This is not only extremely damaging to that person, but the dominant spouse usually starts getting frustrated and bored in the marriage.

A third thing that can happen in a win/lose marriage is divorce. This is when one person finally says "enough is enough" and, sadly, walks away. A win/lose marriage is not a happy or joy filled one, and it will not survive over the long haul.

You have probably heard the saying: "A happy wife is a happy life!" Well, that is true generally. But, ladies, if you are always winning and your husband feels like he is losing in the decisions you make together, he may eventually explode with frustration or check out emotionally. Likewise, gentlemen, if you are so dominant that your wife always feels like she loses, she will stop letting you know what she wants and may also pull away from you in anger or despair.

Instead of orienting your relationship around winning or losing, think and work on creating win/win arrangements. Here's how to do that:

1. **Have an attitude of love**. Think about what you really want in your marriage —which I believe is a strong connection and love. What will make your marriage stronger and bring you closer together? Coming to an agreement, where both of you get what you want, creates a closer bond that lasts over time.

2. **Choose to give and serve**. When you love, give, serve and make your spouse happy, your spouse will want to do the same for you.

3. **Seek to understand.** Instead of focusing on getting your point across or letting your spouse know what you want, pay attention and seek to understand what your spouse wants or needs and why.

4. **Allow your spouse to influence you.** Your spouse sees things differently than you. Accept this and allow them to share their perspective on the situation or decision. Chances are that he or she is seeing something you do not see. Their input can keep you from making a bad decision, but first you must be willing to receive it.

5. **Give up your position so that you can consider new options**. This may sound like losing, but when you hold your desires loosely you are able to create something that is actually better than what you originally desired. Often, it is our pride or selfishness, or simply hating to lose, that causes us to dig in our heels and fight for something that really does not matter. You must first yield or give up your position before you can consider

any new ideas your spouse may want to share with you. When you first yield, you win by getting a closer connection with your spouse and you win when you come up with something that makes both of you happy.

6. **Be creative and think up a third alternative**. If you want to go to McDonald's and your spouse wants to go to Burger King, instead of choosing either of them, you could decide to go to Taco Bell. In other words, why create an option where one person wins and the other loses? Instead, create a choice that the both of you can embrace.

These may sound like small things, but these kind of choices can make or break a marriage over time. When someone in a relationship expresses frustration and anger for not being heard, that concern needs to be taken seriously by their spouse. If it is not responded to appropriately, not only will they feel vulnerable, they will conclude that their desires do not matter. The other common result of win/lose arrangements is the frustration that one person feels when their spouse never has an opinion. This happens when a husband asks his wife what she wants and all he gets is: "Whatever you want, dear."

Learn to like each other

I was talking with a good friend of mine and telling him about my ideas for this book. In response to this subject, he spoke to me about three things that every marriage needs: Love, Like and Longing.

"Love" is the mutual respect, trust and care that you have for another person. I have heard that love desires the highest good for another. "Like" refers to the enjoyment you have by being with someone. You like to be with each other and it does not really matter what you are doing. "Longing," of course, refers to sexual desire in marriage. God created sex and wants us to enjoy it within the context of a lifelong commitment.

Many couples experience two out of three of these elements. They have love and longing, but they do not like each other. Meanwhile, marriages that are in trouble mostly have one out of three. However, you need all three of them in order to have a great marriage and a strong connection. About ten years into his marriage, for example, my friend realized that he and his wife did not really have a lot of things that they liked to do together. So they intentionally focused on correcting that. They began developing mutual interests and things that they both now enjoy doing together. Today, they have been married over forty years and can truly say that they like each other.[3]

Becoming one does not happen accidentally. To have a great marriage, I suggest you make it a top priority to connect with each other. The time you spend together is an investment in your marriage, one that will pay big dividends throughout your life. When you are in the dating or engagement phase of a relationship, this is not much of a challenge because all you can think about is spending time with the person you love. But as time passes, and kids, careers, chores, hobbies and friends demand your time, you will find it easy to neglect your marriage. It is important that you consciously not let that happen. Many couples commit to a date night once a week, for example. When you spend time with each other, it does not really matter when. The point is that you need to be together regularly, talking, sharing, being intimate, having fun and connecting. Spending time with each other is a great way to turn it up.

Develop shared interests

A great way to turn it up and strengthen your connection is to develop shared interests. I have found, from talking to couples that have drifted apart, that one of the common denominators is a lack of shared interests. They started out enjoying many of the same things, but then went in different directions. At times in your marriage, it will be natural to focus on one thing or another. For many, this happens when children enter the equation. For a season, it may be necessary to have a "kid-centric" marriage. Your children will grow up and, if you have done a good job, they will not need you in the same ways as they mature. They will develop other relationships, and will not want you to hang out with them on evenings and weekends. Eventually, they will move away and, ideally, establish their own homes and families. Unfortunately, there are marriages so built around the children that, when they leave the nest, the couple may experience a time when they feel they have nothing in common. They have drifted away from each other and may think they have nothing to keep them together. Separation or divorce does not have to be inevitable in this situation. The key is to cultivate and develop common interests and to connect around mutually enjoyable activities. Couples that have great marriages turn it up by regularly doing things together.

Four categories of activities

You don't have to do everything together. For example, if your wife loves to shop and you hate it, don't try to share this experience regularly. Let her go shopping while you do an activity you enjoy. You can also find something else that you both will like doing. After all, something attracted you to each other in the first place. Think back to that and what you first enjoyed doing together. There will also be things that you may not naturally enjoy; but, because you love your spouse, you make the time and step outside of your comfort zone to share these experiences. Consider these four categories of activities:

Mutual – These are things you both enjoy. For Carrie and I, these include traveling, sightseeing, reading by the pool, and playing with our grandkids.

Companion – These are activities that one of you enjoys, while the other one participates in them just because they have a good time being with you. Shopping usually falls into this category for us, depending on what we are shopping for. House projects, for example, sometimes fall into this category for me. If it were up to me, our home would look the same as it did when we first moved in over twenty years ago. Carrie enjoys doing house projects and is good at them. She enjoys them more when I help her with them, and I enjoy helping her. We mutually benefit from the experience and get to spend time together, building our home and our marriage.

Individual – These are the activities that one of you enjoys, but the other one dislikes. Definitely, golf is in this category for us. I love it, and Carrie thinks it is a waste of time. However, she is okay with me playing it even on vacations, as long as I am not doing it all the time.

Necessary – These are things that neither of you enjoys, but that have to be done. These may include paying bills, cleaning the garage, mowing the lawn --you get the idea. These are not really activities you do to build your connection; but if you don't do them, both your connection and quality of life will suffer. Often, one spouse will be better at one thing than the other, so it is perfectly acceptable to defer to the one who has the greater skill or talent for the particular task.

At different times in life, or when circumstances demand it, one spouse or the other may be required to do things that are not particularly agreeable or pleasant. When the couple is committed to each other, they will find their own way to make things work.

Make it your goal to discover new *mutual* activities and expand that area. By doing new things together, you will find activities that you never thought you would enjoy. When you are doing *companion* activities and are not the one who gets the most out of them, you will find that there is much joy in pursuing your spouse's happiness. *Individual* activities can be beneficial, but don't make these the main focus of your marriage. Golf, for me, will never be the main thing because it is not something that Carrie and I enjoy together. Finally, do not neglect the *necessary* activities. They may not be what you want to spend your time and energy doing on evenings or weekends; but, if you do not address these necessary things consistently, they can become, seemingly, insurmountable and burdensome. This will create problems for the overall health of your marriage.

Strengthen do not damage

Focus on doing things that turn up the connection with each other, instead of what might damage or hinder it. If someone asks me to play golf on Monday, the answer is no, since that is my day to spend time with Carrie. Now, when there are Mondays that she has to work, playing golf is fine. If you want to have a strong connection, think about doing things that will build it and not tear it down. When you just think about what you want to do and not what is best for you as a couple, that is selfishness. Just because I am free to play golf, it does not mean that it is the best thing for me to do. In their book, Boundaries in Marriage, Dr. Henry Cloud and Dr. John Townsend write,

So the Bible's warning offers the best solution for that danger: "Love your neighbor as yourself." In other words, in your exercise of separateness, make sure that you are seeing how your freedom and separateness are affecting your spouse. Would you want to be treated with disregard? Certainly not. Practice the Golden Rule.[4]

The conversations you have while being together will be far more important than the activities you share. In conversation, you will share your heart, feelings, thoughts, and desires, and talk about what is going on in each of your lives. It is important to realize that this connection is not so much about what you do, as it is about the sharing that occurs while you are together. Your husband or wife wants, and needs, to know what is going on in your heart and head, and in your day-to-day life. You want, and need, to know what is going on in theirs. The only way to accomplish that is by talking to each other. The best conversations take place when you are together. Phone calls, emails and texts are okay if you are away from one another, but do not substitute this for the real thing. Nothing beats face-to-face interaction.

Develop good friendships

Believe it or not, one of the ways that will help you to turn it up and become one with your husband or wife is to develop friendships with other same-sex friends. Gentlemen, we need good male friendships; ladies, you need good female friends. There is something special that happens when guys hang out with guys, and when ladies hang out with ladies. Sure, I want to spend the majority of my free time with Carrie. However, occasionally doing something like playing golf or going to see a movie with a good friend actually enhances the time I spend with my wife.

Same sex friends also provide wisdom. When I get frustrated or angry about something, it is really helpful to talk about that challenge with one of my friends, in addition to talking about it with Carrie. As much as I value Carrie's perspective on the issue, getting another guy's point of view is really helpful. Solomon wrote, "For lack of guidance a nation falls, but victory is won through many advisers." (Proverbs 11:14 NIV). The key here is balance. There really can be too much of a good thing. You can spend a lot of time with friends and neglect your spouse, but adding variety to your marriage, by good conversations or activities with friends, can actually strengthen the connection you have with your husband or wife.

Becoming one sexually

Using my friend's outline, all marriages need to have Love, Like and Longing. Longing is desire that is not selfish. The Bible uses the word "lust" to refer to selfish desire. Lust, or selfish desire, doesn't have a place in a great marriage and will damage your connection. In fact, great sex is focused on giving, not on taking from your lover. This is why sex is a gift from God, designed to be experienced in the safety of a married relationship as a way to bring you closer to each other. There is a lot of encouragement from experts to have "safe sex". This usually means not participating in risky sexual behaviors, like not using condoms or having multiple partners. In reality, the only sex that is safe is married sex. Sex is a powerful force. Think of it like fire. Fire can warm your home and cook your dinner, but it can also destroy and damage. Does this make fire good or bad? It depends on how it is used. In the same way, God designed sex to unite a couple and strengthen their connection.

When we talk about married sex we mean intimacy. God's idea of sex is for it to be an experience that connects a husband and a wife spiritually, as well as emotionally and physically. If you ever think that God is embarrassed by sex or that it is not his idea, read the Song of Solomon in the Bible. It is a very poetic, and sometimes graphic, description of physical and sexual intimacy.

You will not have a great marriage or strong connection if you have difficulty uniting sexually. Problems in the bedroom can be caused by a variety of things. Sometimes there is a lack of desire due to stress or worry about something. Other difficulties come when one person's focus is all about taking, and their spouse starts feeling used. If there is a lack of emotional connection in your marriage, having sex can be forced, as one spouse tries to make up for this with physical intimacy. Another reason for sexual challenges is when there has been extramarital sexual activity or adultery. This can be anything from flirting or having physical intimacy with someone other than your spouse, a relationship with an online partner where one engages in sexual language or fantasy, or the use of pornography as a means to sexual fulfillment. A further hindrance to having a healthy sex life is past abuse.

All of these challenges can be dealt and resolved with love and commitment. I encourage you to honestly talk about your feelings surrounding sex in a vulnerable way. When difficulties do arise, it may be appropriate to see a professional to deal with these issues. Great marriages have an active, healthy sexual component. Regular and consistent sex in a marriage will strengthen the connection you have with each other. If that is not the case, it is necessary for the couple to take the steps necessary to correct this. Reading and applying the advice in this book is a great start.

Conclusion

If you want to turn up the connection in your marriage, the first step is to make a lifelong commitment to becoming one with each other. This doesn't just happen automatically. It takes time, planning, resources and effort, but it is worth the work and investment. You really can turn it up in order to have a strong connection and a great marriage when you make this your first commitment to each other: "*I commit to becoming one with you.*" As you do this, you will be amazed on how God will bless you with a great marriage.

With each other:

1. Share what spoke to you the most out of this chapter.

2. Practice making win/win arrangements.

3. Discuss how you can develop more mutual interests so that you can become one with each other.

CHAPTER THREE

COMMITMENT #2

PRIORITIZE, CARE FOR AND

PROTECT YOUR CONNECTION

Because I value our marriage, I commit to prioritizing, caring for and protecting our connection.

When you say your vows to each other or participate in a marriage ceremony, a living entity is created. That entity is your marriage, and it needs your attention. Just like anything that is alive, your marriage needs to be nurtured regularly by turning up and strengthening your connection. If you prioritize, care for and protect your connection, your marriage will thrive and grow strong; and you will have a great relationship that will last. If you neglect your connection, your marriage will weaken, get sick and die. What you love, you value. What you value, you prioritize, care for and protect. When you do this and consistently invest in your marriage by turning up and strengthening it, you will enjoy the blessings of a great one. If you want to have a great marriage, the second commitment I encourage you to make to each other is this: *"Because I value our marriage, I commit to prioritizing, caring for and protecting our connection."*

Prioritize your connection

Is the connection you have with your spouse the top priority in your life? Next to my relationship with God, the top priority of my life is my relationship with my wife. It is the most important human relationship in my life, followed of course by my relationships with my kids and grandkids. As I mentioned in chapter one, Carrie and I monitor the quality of our connection. We are very sensitive to how we are doing as a couple. This doesn't come out of a heart of fear, but as a priority. I want to make sure that we are dealing with the issues or conflicts that arise and resolving them. I also want to ensure we are doing things together that strengthen our connection with each other. When Carrie comes home from work, I turn off the TV, get off the couch and greet her. When she calls while I am at work, with a few exceptions, I always stop what I am doing to answer.

I want her to know by my actions that she is the most important person to me in the whole world. I ask her regularly how she is doing, how things are going at work and what she is concerned about. I want to enter into her world and then share my world with her. I enjoy spending time together and it does not really matter what we are doing. She is my top priority because I love her, and she loves me. When you value something, like your marriage, you automatically prioritize it. Because it is a priority, you then take care of it.

Be proactive

Prioritizing your connection requires that you be both proactive and reactive. To be proactive means you take care of something in advance rather than waiting for it to break down. Much of the concepts in this book are proactive in nature. If you do these things, you will avoid many of the problems and challenges that come within a marriage. It is wise to be proactive and avoid possible challenges, but you also need to be ready to react when your connection hits a speed bump. When you prioritize your connection, you drop everything else and focus on resolving the problem. If he or she is upset with you about something, you need to find out what's wrong and do your best to fix it. Usually, that means apologizing or asking for forgiveness. Why do you do that? Because your connection is your priority; and, because it is your priority, you care for it, nurture it, protect it and do whatever it takes to make it stronger.

Care for your connection by committing to it

If you want to have a great marriage, you must also care for your connection. There are three foundational ingredients to all marriage relationships: commitment, trust and respect. Caring for your connection means you must establish and strengthen these three things consistently, and it starts with the commitment you make to each other on the day you get married. Our pastor, Dr. Jim Reeve, has taught Carrie and me that commitment means, "...abandoning the option to quit."[5] Marriage is for keeps. There is no back door, plan B or escape route. Most wedding vows contain the words, "... till death do us part." That is how you have to look at it in order to make your marriage a great one and to maintain a strong connection.

All marriages have conflicts. Marriage brings out the best in us, but it can also bring out the worst. We are sinful, hurt, broken human beings that hurt others. Not everything will always flow smoothly between the two of you. In those times, you may be tempted to leave. You may even think that getting married was the biggest mistake you ever made. You may consider all the people you know who are divorced, and might even fantasize that your life would be better if you were single again. Do not ever think that a divorce is an option. Do not threaten to divorce when you are angry. Here is what God says about this,

"The man who hates and divorces his wife," says the LORD, the God of Israel, "does violence to the one he should protect," says the LORD Almighty. So be on your guard, and do not be unfaithful." (Malachi 2:16, NIV).

Problems and challenges are a consistent part of human experience. Security and trust in marriage come from knowing that you are committed to each other, and that you will not walk away when things get hard. Because you have abandoned the option to quit, you turn to each other, ask for forgiveness, talk about what happened and why, and seek to resolve the issues. You get help if needed, and do whatever you need to do to turn it up and reestablish your connection. Your spouse is not your enemy; your spouse is your ally. When you have no way out, you work it out.

Care for your connection by establishing trust

Along with commitment, all connections need trust in order to survive and thrive. Trust is the second ingredient in caring for your connection. According to the Miriam Webster Dictionary, trust is, "…the belief that someone or something is reliable, good, honest, and effective."[6] When you trust someone, you believe that they are a good person who will not hurt you and that they will do what they promise. You believe the other person is for you, that they have your back and that they care about you. You feel safe when you are in a marriage with someone you trust. You can relax and be who you really are because you know your spouse has accepted you; and you can live without fear of rejection, shame or criticism. A person you trust is reliable, dependable and good with their words and actions. After years of research in relationships and marriage, the relationship expert Dr. John Gottman says, "The number one thing a woman looks for in a man is simply this: trustworthiness."[7]

Trust does not automatically happen in a marriage. If you have been hurt in the past, especially in a romantic relationship, it may be hard for you to trust. But as you get to know someone, discover their character and see who they really are, you will start to trust that person. You will not be as afraid of getting hurt, as you were at first, and you will drop your guard, little by little.

Trust is absolutely critical in a marriage. When trust is broken, your connection with each other will suffer and your relationship will be in trouble. Trust is developed and earned by being trustworthy, but it is damaged and injured by being untrustworthy. Think of it as a bank account in which you make deposits and withdrawals. When you say you will be home for dinner and you show up on time consistently, your spouse will trust you. You are making a trust deposit. But when you say you will be home for dinner and then show up late without calling, you are making a trust withdrawal. It is crucial to deliver on the things to which you are committing. If you cannot follow through on what you promise, your spouse will learn not to trust you. Learn to make promises carefully and with intent, then be a person who keeps them. This will build trust between the two of you.

In addition to being untrustworthy, the other killer of trust is betrayal. Betrayal is any choice that does not prioritize your commitment to each other or does not put your spouse before everyone else. Whenever you put something or someone ahead of your marriage, you have betrayed your spouse. The example that most people think of is adultery.

Certainly, whenever you have an extramarital relationship, that absolutely is a betrayal. But betrayal can be much more subtle. Whenever your hobbies, work or friendships take priority over your marriage, you have betrayed your husband or wife. Even putting your kids ahead of your spouse is a betrayal. Whenever you side with someone else, perhaps your parents, against your spouse it is also a betrayal. The person you have committed your life to must know that, no matter what happens, you are there for them and you will not let anyone or anything come between the two of you.

Another way spouses betray each other is by being emotionally distant. When you are afraid of sharing how you really feel with your spouse, you are closing yourself off to them. This is also a betrayal because you are choosing to hide. You are choosing to protect yourself, instead of choosing to trust. I realize this can be hard to do if you have been hurt; but choosing to trust and be vulnerable, in order to open up to your spouse, will strengthen your connection and give you the great marriage that you really want.

If you have unintentionally betrayed your spouse, by letting other things become more important to you, by siding with another person against your spouse or by being emotionally distant out of fear, do something about it. Go to your spouse and admit what you have done or allowed to happen. Apologize to them and then start building trust again, by demonstrating that they are the most important person in your life. This is how you turn it up.

Trust comes from telling the truth

Telling the truth is the primary way you build trust. The main reason we lie to each other is because we are trying to manage the outcome or reaction of someone finding out the truth. You may not want your spouse to get mad at you for using your grocery money to buy alcohol, so you lie and tell them that you lost or misplaced it. Some people hesitate to tell the truth because they know it will hurt their loved one. For example, if you don't have the money to pay your electric bill, you may be tempted to lie to your spouse when she or he asks about it. You rationalize this by telling yourself that they may get upset about your financial situation. You justify the lie by getting convinced that you just want to keep the peace or that you do not want to make your spouse mad. When the lights get shut off and the truth comes out, you have made the problem much worse. Instead of just having a financial problem, now you have a trust problem. If your spouse is unable to trust you to tell them the truth in the little things, they will not trust you with the big things. Just as important as making a commitment to abandon the option of quitting, is also making a commitment to always tell the truth to each other, no matter the outcome.

Telling the truth means telling the whole truth. I have learned, the hard way, that not telling the whole truth of a given situation to Carrie is the same as lying to her outright. One time, I got a ticket for not wearing my seatbelt. The police officer told me that it would not go on my record or affect my insurance if I just paid the fine, so I decided it was not important enough to disclose to Carrie. I realized my mistake when, later, I let it slip that I had received this ticket. She got very angry with me and asked, "What else aren't you telling me?" I saw that I had made a significant trust withdrawal. Wow, that hurt, but it opened my eyes. I pride myself on being a man of integrity, and someone who always tells the truth. When I saw that not telling my wife everything was as bad as lying to her, I made the commitment to tell her the whole truth every time. Even though it is hard, I let her know about my mistakes and failures. She knows I am not perfect, but she can trust me. When you tell each other your screw-ups, you are able to support and give grace to one another. When you reveal your mistakes and shortcomings to each other, you actually build trust; you also invite your spouse into the process of your growth and change. Telling the truth and being trustworthy are sure fire ways to strengthen and maintain your connection with each other.

Trust comes from transparency

Another way to build trust is to be totally transparent and tell each other about your contacts with the opposite sex. Be open and invite your spouse to look at your texts, call records, social media posts and emails. On one occasion, I had a desperate man come to me for prayer and advice. He had reconnected with an old girlfriend and they had started texting each other. She was brazen enough to invite him to meet her at a motel. Though he did the right thing and turned her down, he made the critical mistake of not telling his wife. When she looked at his phone and saw texts from another woman, including the invitation to the motel, she considered it a significant breach of trust. She felt that she could no longer trust her husband and considered getting a divorce. It hurt this man deeply. Even though he felt he had done nothing wrong, his marriage was damaged because he was not forthcoming about this situation. After apologizing, asking forgiveness and getting some coaching from me, his wife did forgive him and now he is rebuilding trust with her again. He learned an important lesson that he will not forget.

The point is that when you are married, your phone and computer are no longer off limits. You no longer have any privacy. What is yours is your spouse's, what is theirs is now yours. When you tell each other about everything, suspicion never builds up, trust is developed and significant deposits are made in your trust account. Caring for your connection means you always tell the truth, the whole truth, and live a transparent life with each other. The result is a trusting marriage and a strong connection.

Respect

The third ingredient of caring for your connection is respect. The Apostle Paul, an influential follower of Jesus who wrote a large part of the New Testament, had this to say about how God wants husbands and wives to treat each other. "However, each one of you also must love his wife as he loves himself, and the wife must respect her husband" (Ephesians 5:33, NIV).

I have always found interesting that he tells a husband to love his wife as he loves himself, but he tells wives to respect their husbands. Just as trust is developed in a relationship by making more deposits than withdrawals, respect is earned. To respect someone is to hold that person in high esteem. Another word for respect is admiration. You admire a person, or respect a person, because of how they behave. Getting up every day and going to work so that your family has food on the table and a roof over their heads is a way to earn respect. If you tell the truth and live transparently, you will earn your spouse's respect. You respect a person because of their honesty and integrity, and because they do the right thing. A respected person is not perfect, but they confess their mistakes and then move on. Respect is foundational to creating and maintaining a strong connection with each other.

Wives have the power to make their husbands feel respected

Just as a husband has the power to make his wife feel loved, a wife has the power to make her husband feel respected.

There are a lot of differences between women and men. In my observation, a woman wants to feel special, wanted and loved by her man; while the man wants to be respected and admired by his woman. One way a man finds his identity is in what he does for a living. Often, the first thing men talk about when they meet is their jobs. It can be devastating for a man to be unemployed. It is not just the financial struggle, but being unemployed can damage a man's very identity.

So, wives, if you are tempted to blame your husband, put him down, tell him he is a no good loser or that no one will hire him, you are disrespecting him and undermining his own self-respect. He probably already feels bad enough for not finding work; but when he hears your disappointment, it is demoralizing. Instead, I suggest you hold him in high esteem, build him up and show him that you respect him. When he knows you believe in him and are cheering him on, he will find the courage to go out, fight the feelings of rejection and keep doing what he needs to do to find a job. He will believe in himself and be more confident in those interviews.

Remember that words are powerful. Along with words of love, words of admiration and respect need to be shared with your spouse on a regular basis. They can build up, bless and encourage; but they can also tear down, discourage and destroy your husband or wife. One way to strengthen and care for your connection is to show respect and honor to each other through both your words and actions.

Turn it up!

Show respect by being sensitive

One way to show respect is to be sensitive to the feelings of your spouse. When you are like this, you care about someone and wonder how they are handling the challenges of life. The key to being sensitive is to be aware, and to pay attention to the verbal and nonverbal cues your spouse communicates. I have found that it is very easy for me to get wrapped up in my work, hobbies or even projects around the house. I can get so focused that it may not even register on my radar that my wife is upset about something.

Showing respect and being sensitive is being aware and taking the initiative to ask your spouse how they are doing. Do not wait until they are so mad at you that they decide to bring up the infamous phrase, "we need to talk", because things may have reached a critical stage by then. So look around, listen and train yourself to be sensitive to your spouse's needs and wants, and then respond. Ask questions, hold their hand, show your spouse that you love and care for them. Being sensitive to the feelings of your spouse is another way to monitor your connection. It shows that you care and want to strengthen your connection.

Show respect by giving freedom

You also show respect by giving your spouse freedom. Respect is not controlling or domineering, nor is it forcing the other person to obey you. When your husband or wife disagrees with you, respect is allowing them to have their own opinion on the matter, even if that is different from yours. Respect is allowing your spouse to have a choice, and you should respect that choice —even if it is not what you want or think best. When you show respect, you treat your spouse like an adult that is free to run their own life. If you want to go to the movies and your spouse does not want to, do not pressure or force them to go. They will end up resenting it, you will have a lousy time and maybe even get into a fight over it.[8]

God gave us the gift of free will because he wanted human beings to choose to love him. He respects our choice, even though this means some people choose not to love him. In the same way, we need to give our spouses freedom to choose how to love and connect with us. If they set a boundary and we violate it —by forcing them to do something with guilt and pressure, or by manipulating them in some way— we are not showing them respect.

One of the greatest things to hear are the words "I love you", but those are meaningless if they don't come from a heart that is free to choose love. When you respect someone, you give them freedom to love or to not love. You give them freedom to have their own likes and dislikes, and to do what they want with their lives. When the other person is free to not love you, and later they choose to do so, your marriage will become powerful and you will form a connection that will withstand all the challenges that might come against it.

Protect your connection from outside influences

Another way to turn it up and care for your connection is to protect it from outside influences. Protecting your connection is a very powerful way to keep something form turning it down.

Imagine this scenario: things are not great at home because you and your spouse are having some problems, and you need to work on them. There are some built up feelings of anger and frustration interfering with your connection. Meanwhile,

Turn it up!

at work, you have developed a friendship with a co-worker of the opposite sex. You work well together on projects and he or she is easy to talk to. You discover that you have a lot in common. One day, after having a fight with your husband or wife, you confide in this co-worker. You share your frustration and find yourself feeling much better afterwards; it seems like this person really knows how to listen and help. The two of you have to work late one day, so you bring dinner into your office and eat together. Another time, you two decide to go for lunch. At first, it seems harmless. You say to yourself, "Co-workers do this all the time." But one day you realize you have romantic feelings for them and you are excited to see them at work. Back at home, your husband or wife has noticed that you have been happy, yet distant. You are not really present because you are thinking about something else. As time goes by, you and your co-worker find yourselves spending more and more time with each other. A bond has developed. Then something happens and you accidentally touch. By now, you get the picture, and can imagine what might happen next.

Avoid emotional intimacy with others

The truth is that adulterous affairs don't happen accidentally. People don't accidentally fall in love. The first step to adultery is emotional intimacy with someone other than your spouse. It is critical to realize that you can be intimate with another person without being sexually involved; intimacy is simply developing a close relationship with them. If you value your connection with your spouse, protect it by not getting close to someone of the opposite sex. Do not ever, ever, allow yourself to get emotionally intimate with anyone other than your husband or wife. If you rewind the scenario I presented earlier to one where you decide to talk to a same-sex friend after the fight with your spouse, the outcome would be completely different. If a challenge in your marriage has escalated to a critical level, rather than reaching out to someone of the opposite sex, get help from a pastor, coach or marriage therapist, so that issues can be addressed and resolved without the frustration deepening further. Getting help is not a sign of weakness, it is wisdom.

The best way to avoid emotional intimacy with someone other than your spouse is to never allow it to happen. Set standards or rules for yourself, and follow them. As a pastor who interacts regularly with both men and women, I have a rule for myself: I never go out for lunch with a woman alone. Another no-brainer for me is to always leave my office door open when talking to a woman. It just makes good sense to circumvent any opportunity for misunderstanding or for something unseemly to transpire.

In a work environment you will, most likely, interact with members of the opposite sex regularly. You will develop connections and friendships. Keep those relationships at a professional level by not sharing your deep personal feelings or other information. Do not allow those relationships to go deeper than what is appropriate. If you are not communicating with your spouse about your friendships with the opposite sex at work, you may want to ask yourself why is this the case.

Be careful online

The same thing applies for online friendships. I have spoken to heartbroken people whose spouses left them for someone they met and developed a relationship with online. An old friend from high school sends you a friend request on social media, then he or she sends you a message. You share an online conversation that soon leads to daily chat times and regular emails. It does not matter how innocently it starts: whenever you share your heart with someone, emotional intimacy is developed. Value your spouse and marriage, and you will not be tempted to gamble them away.

A good way to keep from getting into trouble is to use the "Tell your husband or wife about it" test. If you cannot tell your spouse about something you are thinking or doing, because you think it might upset them, then you are already in dangerous territory. Imagine tonight, at dinner, telling your spouse that tomorrow you are going for lunch with your old girlfriend or boyfriend from high school. How do you think they will react? Now apply this to everything else in your life. Your connection is protected when you are open and honest with your spouse.

Avoid pornography

Not only do you need to protect your connection by not developing emotional intimacy with another person, you also need to keep from turning it down by protecting it from sexual fantasies created from exposure to pornography. Due to the Internet, pornography is everywhere and is easily accessible. You just have to turn on your computer in the privacy of your own home. Porn is dangerous and very damaging for you, as well for your connection with someone you love. The Bible uses the term "lust of the flesh" to describe consuming, selfish desire. "For everything in the world—the lust of the flesh, the lust of the eyes, and the pride of life —comes not from the Father but from the world (1 John 2:16 NIV). Jesus also spoke about lust in the Sermon on the Mount: "You have heard that it was said, 'You shall not commit adultery,' but I tell you that anyone who looks at a woman lustfully has already committed adultery with her in his heart" (Matthew 5:27-28 NIV).

Pornography is immoral and destructive because it is based on lust, not love. Lust is a desire that is selfish. It is important to realize that the essence of sin is selfishness. When someone lusts after something, whether it is a piece of cake, a new car or a naked woman, he wants that object to fulfill a selfish desire. Pornography turns men and women into objects of lust. When you look at an image of a naked man or woman on your computer, you are tempted to think of that person as a thing and not as a human being. He or she is someone's son or daughter. You will not consider their personality, only their body. You may be tempted to use their body to get aroused and to gratify yourself. That is not love; it is a cheap substitute. Because it appeals to a selfish and sinful nature, pornography is extremely addicting. All the time I talk to men whose lives are consumed with sex. They have a trail of broken marriages and relationships behind them. They realize they are addicted and say they want to stop. The sad part is that, because they are addicted to porn, they are unable to have a satisfying sexual relationship with a real person —even with their spouse.

Pornography will poison and injure your sexual relationship with your husband or wife, not enhance it. When you pollute your mind with pornographic images and fantasies, you will inevitably compare your spouse to the images you have seen. The body on your computer screen looks perfect. There are no blemishes, warts, problems or defects. The person on your screen is never tired; they do not have bad days, headaches and they never are in a bad mood. The image on your screen is always there to please and satisfy you. The problem is that the image you are enjoying is not real, and what you are feeling is not love. It will be impossible to be intimate with your spouse when you are thinking of someone else, especially an imaginary someone else.

Turn it up!

Because the image on the screen seems perfect, you communicate to your spouse that they are inadequate. When your husband or wife learns that you look at porn, and it is just a matter of time before they find out, it may make him or her feel insecure. They will wonder if they measure up to the fantasy in your mind. Porn will contaminate your sex life with them. This is true for women as well as for men. Here is what a man wrote about his wife, who was addicted to porn:

> Many of the effects are the same [as what wives of porn addicts feel], including feelings of inadequacy and fear that I am not capable of fulfilling my wife's needs.

> I am also afraid that she doesn't really want me sexually. It affects my health profoundly, and I am suffering daily with fear and battling depression. I am living in fear that she will cheat on me, and she has trouble telling me that she will not. When I have an episode where I can't get an erection, she says many hurtful things and threatens to get satisfied elsewhere. This, in turn, increases the frequency of the performance anxiety...

> Sex is an intensely mental state and, if fear or doubt is involved, arousal is impossible... She refuses to believe this, because it is coming from me and I am just blaming my problem on her. She says that I am not attracted to her and that maybe she needs to find someone who is. This is not the case. I am attracted to her; yet mentally I am in turmoil, not able to focus on anything but doubt.[9]

Turning to porn when you do not feel satisfied with the sexual relationship in your marriage will damage both you and your spouse. It will worsen any problem that could have been mended with the guidance from a therapist, along with the trust and respect from and for your spouse.

Another terrible effect porn has in a marriage is that couples find themselves avoiding sex altogether. It is such painful territory that they are seldom intimate with each other. As I have said before, sex is a gift from God that brings you closer to your spouse. You turn things up in your marriage when you protect your sex life. God really wants you to have a great and satisfying sex life with your spouse. The way you protect your sex life is by focusing your attention on the person to whom you have committed. "Marriage should be honored by all, and the marriage bed kept pure, for God will judge the adulterer and all the sexually immoral" (Hebrews 13:4 NIV). Keeping the marriage bed pure means not allowing anything to come into your heart or head; not another person, nor a computer image to take the place of your spouse and impair your ability to enjoy and be intimate with each other.

One of the biggest lies from the devil is that, when you limit yourself to only one sex partner for life, you will get bored. The truth is that, when you are faithful to your spouse, your sexual experiences with them will just get better and better as time passes. Solomon, the wisest man who ever lived and author of Proverbs, put it this way: "May your fountain be blessed, and may you rejoice in the wife of your youth. A loving doe, a graceful deer —may her breasts satisfy you always, may you ever be intoxicated with her love" (Proverbs 5:18-19 NIV).

The path to what you desire, a great marriage and sex life, is not through counterfeit, illicit or extramarital sex. It is through being committed to the connection with your spouse, guarding and protecting your marriage from all outside influences. Refuse to let another person, idea or image into your life or your heart to take the place of your spouse. Guard yourself and protect your connection.

Overcoming sexual addiction

If you, or your spouse, are struggling with a sexual addiction, avoiding sexual intimacy or your marriage has been damaged by pornography, it is time to seek help. The gift from God, given to draw you closer to each other, has been corrupted and needs repair. If you brought this ruin into your marriage, it is important that you confront the issue. Sexual addictions do not just go away, and you need help to stop.

The first step is to stop denying you have a problem. Step One of the Twelve Steps says, "I admit that I am powerless over my addiction and that my life has become unmanageable."[10] Face the reality that you have a sexual addiction, and that you cannot stop by yourself. Believe it or not, admitting you are powerless is the key to freedom. When you realize you cannot beat this on your own, you will do whatever it takes to overcome it. The next thing is to ask for forgiveness from your spouse. Take responsibility for the damage you have done to your marriage, and ask them to forgive you and support you in your recovery. Then seek help from others. This can be with a therapist; although, along with that, you may want to join a support group for those who struggle with sexual addictions.

You may think that your struggle is not an addiction because you only do it occasionally. Try to stop consuming pornography on your own. If you can, then you are probably not addicted but just need support to stay clean. If you are unable to stop, then you are addicted, and you need to admit it to yourself and a group of fellow strugglers. You will find acceptance, grace, truth, structure and accountability within a group. With their support, you will overcome this challenge. Addictions can be defeated, but you cannot do it on your own. Once you are "free", realize that you will always have this area of weakness in your life. Just like an alcoholic who has been sober for twenty years or more, not able to allow himself even one drink or he will relapse, you must never ever allow yourself to consume pornography again.

Not only will you need recovery, but your sexual relationship with your spouse is going to need major rehabilitation if you are going to have the joy God intends for you in marriage. A few visits with a therapist will help along with books and articles made to guide you in restoring sexual intimacy within your marriage. Do not despair, God can and will heal and restore what has been damaged —if you do your part.

Feed your connection regularly

Another way to turn it up is to feed your connection regularly. Do not wait until you are in trouble before you start investing in your marriage. Do not wait until it is starving to feed it. Tend to your connection as you would a garden. Living things need to eat to live. You don't just eat once a week, or even once a year. If you are like me, you need to eat and also like to eat every day. My point is that you need to feed and nourish your connection on a regular consistent basis. A great way to do so is by spending time together and developing common interests, like we talked about in the last chapter.

In the following chapters, we will talk about other ways to feed your connection, such as sharing your feelings, learning more about how to be married and demonstrating your love regularly. By doing these things, you are investing in your connection. Just like in any good investment, you build equity over time. Carrie and I have invested a lot in our marriage, and continue to feed it for it to remain strong. The dividends of this investment and feeding our connection are what contributes to a great marriage.

Conclusion

You can have a great marriage and turn up its strength if you commit to prioritizing, caring for and protecting your connection. I encourage you to make this commitment: *"Because I value our marriage, I commit to prioritizing, caring for and protecting our connection."*

Caring for your connection starts by making a commitment: to abandon the option to quit. It means trusting and respecting each other, being transparent and honest, and telling the truth and protecting your connection from outside influences. You really can have a great marriage when you care for your connection. When you prioritize, care for and protect your marriage, you also get to enjoy it.

With each other:

1. Talk about why commitment, trust and respect are so important to a marriage.

2. What are some ground rules you could put in place to protect your marriage from outside influences?

3. Many relationships have been devastated by pornography. If yours has, talk about what you can do to repair the damage, get help and rebuild the intimacy in your marriage. What actions do you need to take right now? If your marriage has not been impacted by pornography, what practical steps can you take to prevent that from happening?

CHAPTER FOUR

COMMITMENT #3 DEMONSTRATE
YOUR LOVE FOR EACH OTHER

I commit to showing you regularly that I love you

When I perform a wedding ceremony, I include some words of instruction, as well as some thoughts for the couple to think about before they share their vows. I present one of these challenges in a humorous way that usually gets a chuckle out of the audience. I challenge the couple to "love each other", which seems like an obvious thing to say when they are about to get married. If they did not love each other, they would not be doing it. I have learned that it is not enough to have love in your heart for someone, you also need to let them know that they are loved. This is done through both our words and our actions. If you want to have a great marriage or relationship, then you need to turn it up and strengthen the connection you have with each other. A great way to do so is to regularly demonstrate to your spouse, through actions, that you love him or her. I encourage you to make the third commitment. *"I commit to showing you regularly that I love you."*

Loving is giving

As I challenge the couple to love each other, I give them a phrase that I hope they remember: "Loving is giving." To show or express your love for one another, you give to the one you love. When my pastor, Dr. Jim Reeve, talks about finances, he says, "You can give without loving, but you can't love without giving."[11] Pastor Jim's context for this statement is in the area of financial giving to God, but the application extends into the marriage relationship. As part of the marriage ceremony, I read this scripture to the couple: "Do nothing out of selfish ambition or vain conceit. Rather, in humility value others above yourselves, not looking to your own interests but each of you to the interests of the others." (Philippians 2:4, NIV).

Then I say: "What this means, (groom's name), is that when you come home from a hard day at work, do not just plop down on the couch and say, 'Where is my wife? I need her to cook my dinner, get me something to drink, or rub my tired feet.' No, what this verse means is that you get up off the couch or perhaps don't even sit down. Ask yourself, 'Where is my wife?' You need to make sure her needs are met before your own. You need to look for ways to serve her, give to her and make her the happiest woman on earth."

At this point, the bride usually has a big smile on her face. So, I turn to her and say: "Now, (bride's name), before you think this is the best deal in town, (then I pause a moment for a chuckle from the audience, which most of the times I get), it works the same for you. Do not just come home from a hard day, plop down on the couch and look for your husband to meet your needs. Instead, seek to meet his needs before your own. Your goal is to make him the happiest man on earth."

In God's plan for marriage, each of us is to put the needs of our spouse before our own. The beauty of this is that, as my wife focuses on meeting my needs and I focus on meeting hers, we are both happier. A great way to turn it up and strengthen your connection is to focus on what you can give to your spouse rather than focusing on what you can receive. You express your love by giving, serving and meeting his or her needs. Remember: loving is giving, and your love needs to be demonstrated to each other regularly. How do you do that?

Be a servant

One day, two of Jesus' disciples were arguing about who was going to be the greatest in Jesus' kingdom. Jesus replied with one of the most astounding and counterintuitive statements in the Bible:

> And Jesus called them to him and said to them, "You know that those who are considered rulers of the Gentiles lord it over them, and their great ones exercise authority over them. But it shall not be so among you. But whoever would be great among you must be your servant, and whoever would be first among you must be the slave of all (Mark 10:42-44, NIV).

In the movies, we have all seen how kings or government leaders act. They give orders. They are served and waited upon by others. The famous response given to the king by his servants is, "Your wish is my command!" Jesus taught that the pathway to greatness in his kingdom is to be a servant. By applying this to marriage, the way to be a great husband or a great wife is to be a servant.

Men, we may think that, because the Bible teaches that we are the head of the house, our wives are our servants. What God wants you to do, and what I am echoing, is that you be the head servant. Jesus modeled this when he washed his disciple's feet. God modeled this by giving his only son so that we might be saved. The most well-known verse in the Bible says: "For God so loved the world, that he gave his only Son, that whoever believes in him should not perish but have eternal life" (John 3:16 NIV). Loving is expressed in giving. God gave his son, Jesus, who then gave his life, so that we could be forgiven of our sin, have a relationship with God and receive the gift of eternal life. In the same way, rather than focusing on what you can get out of a relationship, focus on what you can give. Servants take the initiative. When I am at a restaurant, I always appreciate when my server fills my water glass or refills my drink without me asking for it. Good waiters know that their job is to anticipate the needs of their guests and meet those needs before they are asked. In the same way, try to anticipate the needs of your spouse and respond before he or she has to express them.

Actions, not just words

God did this for us. He not only said he loved us, he demonstrated that love. "But God demonstrates his own love for us in this: while we were still sinners, Christ died for us" (Romans 5:8 NIV). I love the word "demonstrated." Love includes actions, as well as words. After all, how do you know someone means what they say? We see them demonstrate it by what they do. In the same way, while it is important to say "I love you," we must exhibit it daily. The way we do this is by being kind, considerate and helpful. We demonstrate our love by serving. Loving really is giving. You can have a great marriage when you give of your time, your talent, your treasure, your heart and your actions.

We serve and give by asking ourselves: "How can I take what I have been given to enrich the life of my spouse?" All of us have different gifts, talents, skills and abilities that God wants us to use to serve others, including our spouse. There are things that you are not so good at, compared to someone else. There are things that the husband can do better than his wife, and vice versa. Generally speaking, men have more upper body strength than women. Meanwhile, women tend to be more relational. When kids fall down and get hurt, they usually run to the gentler parent, whether it is mom or dad. Gender roles in our culture may set us up to play specific parts in our marriages, but each of us has things to contribute to the family.

Take on household tasks

One way to demonstrate your love to your spouse is to take on tasks that are, out of necessity, repeated on a daily, weekly or monthly basis. Cooking the meals, doing the dishes, taking care of the laundry and mowing the lawn, for example, have to be done regularly to keep the home happy and healthy. Television shows from the nineteen fifties used to show a stay-at-home wife and a breadwinner husband, stereotypically. The good wife would handle all of the house chores so that, when the hard working husband got home, he could relax with the newspaper or the TV before being served a delicious home-cooked dinner. Then, on the weekends, he would get out the lawnmower and do the "hard" job.

Though that picture of the ideal marriage changed over time, many men still expect their wives to do all the housework, manage all the childcare needs and work full-time jobs. If both of you are working, divide up the household duties evenly. As a team, decide who does what to maintain the comfort and stability of your home. Do not use gender stereotypes to make these decisions, but divide up the household tasks by asking these questions: Who wants to do it? Who is better at it? Who likes doing it?

When you share the load equally, neither of you will feel burdened or overwhelmed by all the things that need to be done. When Carrie and I got married, we discussed who was going to do what in our home. Carrie loves to cook, so it was a given that she would be responsible for meals. I grew up in a home where both parents worked to pay the bills. My mom and dad had agreed that one of them would cook dinner and the other would clean up afterwards. Watching my parents share the load, financially and practically, made a huge impact on the way I saw my role as a husband. So, since Carrie was going to do most of the cooking, I offered to do the cleanup. We also discovered that, just because someone enjoys something in one context, it does not mean they might enjoy it in another. When we first got married, Carrie worked as the assistant to the financial controller of a large electrical contracting company. She managed their finances and balanced their accounts every month. I figured that, since she could do it for them, she could do it for us. But, after handling the budget of a big company all day, she didn't want to keep on doing it at home. I agreed to take over this task to everyone's benefit.

Another thing that Carrie loves is decorating and doing home improvement projects. Since early in our marriage, she takes the lead in that department and I assist. She creates the "honey-do" list and we do the projects together. On our honeymoon, she encouraged me to take some of the cash we received as gifts to buy tools. Little did I know that I would be using those tools to do all kinds of things around our house.

Do what you say you will do

Continue to demonstrate your love for each other by following through on what you have committed to do. No one wants to nag or to be nagged. Do not put off the chores you have taken responsibility for, but do them cheerfully and with a servant's heart as an act of love. As you divide up these chores, adjust them so that everyone wins. Remember that your situation in life will change over the course of your marriage, and your role around the house may need to be adjusted. When Carrie went to college, I took on just about everything around the house. I cooked, cleaned and took care of the kids. Our meals were not the best, but no one went hungry.

Do extra things just because

Give back to your spouse by doing spontaneous things that will bless him or her. If your spouse gets home from the grocery store, help them carry in the groceries. When you get up in the morning, you can make the coffee for both of you. Besides these considerate actions, think of sending cards or flowers to their work, surprising them with small, but thoughtful, gifts, or putting caring notes in their lunch bag. The unexpected little things speak for themselves. Carrie and I call these things "just because" gifts. These seemingly insignificant things have the power to delight both the giver and the receiver. They show that you think of each other, know each other, and desire good things for each other.

It's not what, but how

You may have heard the maxim, "It's not what you say, but how you say it." In the same way, "It's not just what you do that counts, but how you do it." Both our actions and our words reflect our hearts. When you love someone, your servant's heart comes out automatically. If you think of your spouse as your servant, someone that is there just to make you happy, your selfishness is going to come out. Be a true partner and friend to them. Assist your spouse in the things they do; not because you have to, but because you want to.

What if your marriage is struggling? What if you do not have feelings of love as much as you used to? Sometimes, you have to "fake it till you make it". Do not be led or controlled by your feelings, but by your commitments. If you are committed to regularly showing your spouse that you love them, it is only natural that sometimes you will not feel like serving or giving. When you do it anyway, you will find that feelings mostly follow actions. Act like you love your spouse, and your actions will usually create the feelings of love you desire.

What if you feel like you are the only one giving? It is hard to serve and give when there is hurt, resentment, anger or an unresolved problem. If your marriage is in significant trouble, you might not be able to fake it. I would recommend you to sit down and talk to your spouse if either of you is having trouble with expressing love in word or deed. Additionally, as stated before, a wise person seeks help when he or she doesn't know what to do. Reach out as soon as you or your spouse expresses the need, sooner rather than later, so that things can be solved and your marriage restored as soon as possible.

Speak your spouse's love language

When you commit to regularly showing your spouse that you love them, it is important that your actions communicate love. In his book *The Five Love Languages,* Dr. Gary Chapman makes this point: what you think that communicates love, may not be the same for your spouse. You and your spouse are different, and each of you has your own love language.

Dr. Chapman has identified five different ways that individuals give and receive love. These are: 1.) Quality Time; 2.) Acts of Service; 3.) Words of Affirmation; 4.)

Receiving Gifts; and 5.) Physical Touch.[12] You will need to discover your spouse's love language, in order to say and do the right things when communicating love to them. Carrie feels loved when I spend quality time with her; and I feel loved when Carrie does acts of service and when she expresses her appreciation for me. If you don't know your spouse's love language, you will try to communicate in your own love language. For example, if receiving gifts is important to you, then you will probably give lots of gifts to your spouse. But, if he or she feels loved when you spend time with them, they would rather have you home than out there shopping for gifts or working all the time to afford those. To turn it up and strengthen your connection, so that you can have a great marriage, you need to express your love in ways that are understood by each other all the time. You will receive much satisfaction by knowing that your spouse feels loved.

Conclusion

Remember that the word *love* is both a noun and a verb. It is an action word, as well as a feeling. And love begets love. When your spouse feels loved, because you regularly demonstrate your love, he or she will desire that you feel loved too. The commitment I encourage you to make in this chapter is: "I *commit to showing you regularly that I love you*". When you do this, you will be turning up your connection, which will not only get stronger but stay strong. By demonstrating your love through actions, you really will see great things happen in your marriage.

With each other:

1. Since loving is giving, what things does your spouse do that demonstrates his or her love for you? Share those things with each other.

2. Talk about how you will divide your household tasks when you get married. If you already are married, examine how your household tasks are usually taken care of. Adjust the responsibilities if needed, so that both of you are satisfied with the arrangement.

3. Ask each other this question: "Is there something I could do to make your life easier?" Talk about how and when you will start doing those things.

4. Complete this sentence, "I feel loved when..." Share what you think your love language is and how your spouse can speak it more fluently to you.

CHAPTER FIVE

COMMITMENT #4

KEEP LEARNING HOW TO TURN IT UP

I commit to learning how to turn it up

The Beatles once wrote a song saying that all you need is love. Most people would probably agree that love is all you need to have a great marriage or relationship. They believe that, if you love each other, everything will be great and all your problems will magically resolve in a cloud of blissful emotion. Love is crucial, but you also need to learn how to turn it up in order to have a great marriage. I have learned in life that nothing just happens. The book you are reading, the chair or sofa you are sitting on, the room you are sitting in to read this, none of these things just happened. Being in a relationship is a lot of work, but the saying goes: "Do not just work hard, work smart." You work smart at your job by learning new ways of doing things that make you more efficient and effective. The same is true when it comes to marriage. I encourage you to be a learner in the arena of love.

You do not have to be ignorant or unequipped. Anyone, even you, can have a great marriage. However, there are things you have to learn for this to be possible. Although there are no guarantees, the more you learn how to turn it up and strengthen your connection —and the more you apply what you learn—, the better prepared you will be to handle the storms of life that can hit your relationship. The fourth commitment I encourage you to make is: "*I commit to learning how to turn it up.*"

Realize you do not know it all

In order to learn how to turn it up, you need to first realize that there are things you do not know. All of us, at times, make the mistake of assuming we know how things work or how they are done. We assume we can figure them out on our own. However, when you live in the world of "I know," you close yourself off to learning new things. If you are honest with yourself, there are some things that you can learn. There are also some lessons to make your journey more enjoyable and easier, of which you are not aware. Be open. Be teachable. Be willing to learn new ways to turn it up and, thus, to have a great marriage. Solomon says: "Let the wise hear and increase in learning and the one who understands obtain guidance." (Proverbs 1:5 NIV).

Some of the things you need to learn are how to demonstrate your love, how to communicate effectively, how to understand your spouse, how to share your feelings and how to resolve conflicts. Having a great marriage takes knowledge, wisdom and skill. Knowledge is information. You need to know things about yourself, about your spouse, and about how to connect with each other. Wisdom is knowing how and when to apply that information. Skill is the ability you develop to actually do what wisdom tells you needs to be done.

Learn from your experiences

There are three ways to get wisdom: from your own experiences, from other's experiences, or from buying it.[13] Learning from your own experiences is all about taking the time to reflect on the daily things that happen, and realizing that some are helpful and others are not. There are actions that can totally make your spouse's day, like bringing flowers, doing dishes, or taking care of the kids while they do something fun with their friends. Certain things that you do for your spouse will be received with appreciation. Meanwhile, things like failing to call when you are going to be late, leaving your clothes on the bedroom floor or not helping around the house will not be appreciated. It is not rocket science, it is common consideration of your spouse. Look for and make mental notes of what makes your spouse happy, and remember to do those things.

In addition to what you do or not do for your spouse, you also need to learn that there are ways to treat your spouse, some which are helpful in turning it up and some that are not. If your natural reaction to your spouse's confrontation is to get defensive, make excuses, blame others or get angry, you will find that it makes the situation worse rather than better. You will have to learn some things the hard way, no doubt. The key is to learn from your experiences and respond in ways that strengthen your connection and turn it up.

A great way to learn from your experiences is to write about them. I keep a journal; in which I write almost every day. Journaling is a great way to reflect on what happens in your life and how you react to those things. Writing about how everything is going in your marriage is a way to examine, not just what you did or said to your spouse that made them mad, but what was going on in your head at the time. Was something triggered inside of you? Did the way he or she spoke to you remind you of how your dad treated you as a child? When you journal about something, you can ask yourself: "Why did I react that way?" When you write about an event or conversation, you have the opportunity to change the future. While you cannot change the past, you can learn from it as you evaluate it. When you evaluate and learn from your experiences, you can then write a new script for the next time you encounter that situation. Experience does not automatically make you wiser, but when you evaluate, learn and apply the knowledge from your experience, you can change the outcome of or possibly even avoid future conflicts or misunderstandings. I encourage you to take the time to reflect and learn from your mistakes. You are not doomed to repeat the failures of your past. God has given you the ability to learn, grow and do things differently next time.

Learn from others

A second way to gain wisdom and knowledge is to learn from others, especially from couples in great marriages. In the early days of our marriage, Carrie and I went to a Sunday school class for newly married couples. This helped us get off to a great start. The combination of lessons from the class leader, plus the interaction and support from the other participants who were often going through the same things we were, truly strengthened our marriage. Perhaps your church offers groups or classes about marriage; if so, by going and participating you will get some great food for your relationship. You could also seek out and meet with couples that have been married longer than you, in order to talk about what they do to make their marriages work.

If you start having significant problems in your marriage, get help from experts. This may include your pastor, professional coach or therapist. When medical problems are addressed early, they can usually be dealt with and corrected; the same is true with relationship struggles. If you begin to experience problems when connecting with each other, you need to get help sooner rather than later. Ignoring or denying a problem will not make it go away, and time doesn't heal all wounds. In fact, ignoring a problem usually makes it worse. There is no shame in acknowledging that you need help. Wise people know they don't have all the answers and seek help from others regularly.

Another way to learn from the experience of others is by attending seminars, retreats and church services that teach marriage principles. Over the years, Carrie and I have been blessed to hear some great speakers at our church that have fed and strengthened our marriage. The best of these teachers are our pastors, Jim and Marguerite Reeve. They have taught us principles to live by and have become role models for us.

You can also get good teaching on marriage through webinars and podcasts. You can search online for speakers, or just type "marriage podcasts" in a search engine. Personally, I subscribe to several podcasts on various topics that are automatically downloaded to my phone. I can listen to them at my convenience, in the car, working around the house and even when I am working out. I encourage you to avail yourself of the multitude of opportunities to learn from others, either in person or via multimedia.

Invest in yourself – buy wisdom

The third way to gain knowledge and wisdom is to buy it. I encourage you to invest both money and time in your relationship by purchasing and reading books like this one. Discuss the things you read, then apply them to your marriage for mutual benefit. One book that Carrie and I read together was *How We Love* by Milan and Kay Yerkovich. This book looks at the different styles that individuals have for expressing and experiencing love. Often, our styles clash, especially if we don't understand our differences. These authors use the illustration of dancing, where one partner keeps stepping on the feet of the other. When you are not in sync, that is what happens. When you learn the love style of your spouse, you can understand each other and experience harmony.[14] I recommend this book to many of the couples I encounter in my ministry.

Another book we found helpful was the one I mentioned in the last chapter, *The Five Love Languages* by Gary Chapman. We learned that each of us has a different way of saying "I love you." If you do not understand nor speak the love language of your spouse, they will feel unloved. When you learn your husband or wife's love language, you can share your love in a way that is understood by them. Of course, the same is true when your spouse understands your love language. Read books together, discuss them, feed and nourish your marriage.

I have included a recommended reading list in Appendix B. These are books I have enjoyed and benefited from greatly.

Another way to invest in your marriage is to hire a coach. Coaching is not counseling or therapy. Many of the couples that I help do not need therapy but simply need to learn new ways of relating to each other. Coaching is a cooperative process that will help you get where you want to go, which is having a great marriage and turning up your connection.

Learn new skills

In addition to gaining knowledge and learning wisdom, you also need to develop some skills that will turn up and strengthen your connection. Skills are things you learn to do and practice over time. When one masters a skill, they have learned to do something well. Knowing what to do and how to do it in a marriage cannot be overstated. Not everything in a marriage can be boiled down to learning skills, but a lot of things can. Some of the things that will help you have a great marriage are things you will simply need to commit to. That is why this book has five commitments, as well as five skills to learn.

Skills do not, however, come naturally. They have to be learned. Most of us think that being married is not something you need to learn how to do. I have talked to many people who have had one failed relationship after another, wondering what is wrong with themselves. People like this tend to feel they are unlucky in love, unable to love or be loved. They may not see their part in the failure, nor acknowledge things they could have learned about their spouse or about marriage that could have helped them to be successful. Their relationship may have failed because one or both parties did not possess the skills needed to sustain a great relationship.

One of the saddest songs I have ever heard is "Just Once", written and performed by Quincy Jones, then later by James Ingraham. In it, the singer shares that he does not know what he and his lover are doing wrong in their relationship. They both want to make it work, but just do not know how. As a result, their relationship seems to be falling apart. In my coaching practice, I often focus on simply helping couples to learn the skills they need to succeed. By doing this, I have seen marriages turn completely around.

Because you and your spouse are committed to turning it up and strengthening your connection, you will be focused on acquiring the skills you need to have a great marriage. Your commitment and character will form the foundation for your motivation to grow and learn with this other person. A heart of love and devotion to your spouse, along with the mutual desire to build a lifelong connection, will make it easier for you to develop the necessary skills for a great marriage —even when the path is difficult.

When I use the word "skill", I usually think of two areas of life where these are developed and used: construction and sports. When you see a gifted athlete or a skilled carpenter, it is natural to think that those abilities just happened in that person's life. "They were obviously born that way! We fail to see the hours or years that someone invested in learning how to shoot a basketball, hit a baseball or drive a nail. We do not see the time spent practicing, practicing, practicing drills, or receiving further coaching or mentoring. Just like an athlete or a contractor, you and your spouse will need to develop your knowledge, wisdom and skills to have the kind of marriage you want.

I encourage you to make learning how to be married a lifelong pursuit. Great marriages do not just happen. They take work, lots of it; and not just hard work, but smart work. Learn how to turn it up and then keep learning. Otherwise, you will never have this figured out. Be proactive. Study and apply together what you learn, so that you can turn it up. Make it an ongoing pursuit of your life together. A wise person doesn't wait until it is raining to repair their roof; they work on it while the weather is good, so that it will be ready for the storms of life.

Conclusion

I hope you are seeing a theme within these first few chapters. Having a strong connection, in order to have a great marriage, is not something that just happens. It takes two committed people, willing to learn and grow together who will turn it up and do the work to get the life that they want. Your efforts will produce positive results as you build the connection that you will enjoy for a lifetime. Making a commitment to learning how to turn it up will bring great dividends. It is a great investment of your time and energy, and a lot of fun too. Make the commitment to be a lifelong learner of how to love someone. *"I commit to learning how to turn it up."*

With each other:

1. Why is it important to realize you do not know it all when it comes to marriage?

2. What are some practical steps you would like to take, so you can learn from your experiences with each other and turn it up?

3. Take a look at the recommended readings page and pick the next book you would like to read.

CHAPTER SIX

COMMITMENT #5

LOVE GOD AND ASK HIM FOR HELP

I commit to loving God and asking him to help us turn it up.

Perhaps the most important commitment you can make, if you wish for a strong connection and a great marriage, is to have a relationship with God. I am not talking about being religious or going to church. I am talking about having a genuine love relationship with your Creator. He loves you, cares for you, and wants to bless your life and marriage; but the choice is up to you. God will not insert himself into your life unless you invite him.

There are a lot of reasons why you need God, and wanting to have a great marriage or relationship is a really good one. The last of our five commitments is: *"I commit to loving God and asking him to help us turn it up."*

God created you and wants to bless you

Why do we need God in our lives? How can he help us to turn it up in our marriage or relationship, in order to have a strong connection? You may not believe in God's existence. However, there are a lot of good books and resources which deal with this topic in a much better way than I could in the scope of this book. If this describes you, I encourage you to examine the evidence for the existence of God and to consider that he might just want to have a relationship with you. It is such an important topic to settle for yourself, especially before you enter into a lifelong relationship with another human being. The Bible gives this reassurance to us: "You will seek me and find me when you seek me with all your heart." (Jeremiah 29:13, NIV).

For our purposes, I will assume that we agree on this: God does exist and he is not just some force in the universe. He reveals himself in both creation and in the Bible. The first reason why loving God will be great for your connection is because He created you and knows you better than you know yourself. He knows your needs, wants and desires, so he is aware of what is best for you. He also has a plan and destiny for your life that he wants to lead you into. Finally, because he loves you, he wants to bless you.

The Bible describes his love for us as the same that a father has for his kids. Jesus said: "If you, then, though you are evil, know how to give good gifts to your children, how much more will your Father in heaven give good gifts to those who ask him!" (Matthew 7:11 NIV). As a broken, sinful and finite human being, I enjoy giving gifts to my kids. How much more do you think our heavenly Father, who is loving, kind and wise, wants to bless his kids with good things? The way we receive these blessings is by first being connected with him through a relationship.

God is the author of love

God is also the author of love. If you want a loving marriage, then being connected with him is the best way to discover what love is all about. Think of it this way: the closer you get to God, the closer you will get to your spouse and the stronger your connection will be. I'm suggesting that the most important relationship in your life needs to be with God, followed by the one you have with your husband or wife. When someone asked Jesus what the greatest commandment was, he quoted a verse from the book of Deuteronomy. "Love the Lord your God with all your heart and with all your soul and with all your mind and with all your strength" (Mark 12:30 NIV). I encourage you to do the same: love God, not your spouse, with all your heart, mind, soul and strength.

We think that it is best to love our husband or wife first, above all else, but that is not what God tells us to do. By loving him with everything you have, you will be blessed and then he will bless your marriage. When you have that relationship with God, he fills your life with love, and that same love later overflows to your spouse. John, one of Jesus Christ's disciples, wrote: "We love because he first loved us." (1 John 4:19 NIV).

When you love God, you are able to love your spouse in ways that transcend the natural love you already have for them. It all starts by first responding to the love that God has for you.

A scripture often shared in weddings is:

> Two are better than one because they have a good return for their labor: If either of them falls down, one can help the other up. But pity anyone who falls and has no one to help them up. Also, if two lie down together, they will keep warm. But how can one keep warm alone? Though one may be overpowered, two can defend themselves. A cord of three strands is not quickly broken (Ecclesiastes 4:9-12 NIV).

God wants to be involved in your marriage. He wants to be the third strand of the cord that is not easily broken.

When you sin against your spouse, you sin against God

Another reason to love God first is because we need his grace, strength, mercy and forgiveness. In the story of Joseph, in the Bible, the wife of his master tries to seduce him. What he says is of extreme importance. "No one is greater in this house than I am. My master has withheld nothing from me except you, because you are his wife. How then could I do such a wicked thing and sin against God?" (Genesis 39:9 NIV). Notice how Joseph is most concerned that the action of adultery with his master's wife would be a sin against God. When treating others badly, we not only sin against that person: we sin against God.

I have lost track of all the times when the Holy Spirit has convicted me of something that I said or did that hurt my wife or my marriage. After those moments, I need to first ask God for his forgiveness, then seek it from my wife. When we live connected to God, he not only fills us with a love that we are able to share with others; he guides us so that we treat others in the way that he wants. When I get off track, he convicts me and shows me what I have done wrong. This is not to condemn me, but to guide me into cleaning that up by asking forgiveness. Because I love God and he loves me, I want to do things that please him. A way that I do this is by treating my wife with love, honor and respect. One of the reasons I am careful about my interactions with other women is because I love God and I love my wife.

Abundant Life

Without a doubt, having a relationship with God through Jesus Christ is the best thing anyone can ever experience. My favorite Bible verse is: "The thief comes only to steal and kill and destroy; I have come that they may have life and have it to the full" (John 10:10 NIV). The full life that Jesus is talking about only comes when you know and follow him, living according to his way and plan. Theologians like Augustine and philosophers like Pascal have taught us that we have a God-shaped vacuum within our souls.[15] There is an emptiness in your life, one that only a relationship with God can fill. He created you to want and need him.

Whenever you feel that emptiness, though, you will want to fill it as best as you can. Some people try to fill that hole with money, power, pleasure or possessions; others even do it with their marriage or families. One of the things I usually mention, during the weddings I conduct, is that your spouse can never be your God. Only God can fill that vacuum and give you true satisfaction, love, joy and peace. When he fills your life with love, he gives it in abundance for you to share with your husband or wife. When you try to convert your spouse into your God, you place extremely unrealistic expectations on them. You are basically saying, "Your job is to make me happy, fulfilled, and to meet all my needs." No human being can do this for you: only God can. When you make Jesus the Lord of your life, he fills that hole and completes you. When you are full of the life that God has for you, you can then share it with the ones you love.

Crazy ways of responding to God's love for you

Gentlemen, imagine the first time you said "I love you" to your wife. How would you feel if she did not reply at first? What if she wasn't sure what to say? That would surely be a scary moment for you, as you waited and wondered: "Is she going to reject me? Is she going to say she is not sure of her feelings for me? Or is she going to say 'I love you, too'?"

When she eventually does say the words you were hoping for, you will breathe a sigh of relief. In the same way that you wanted for this girl, who you had fallen in love with, to respond to your love, God wants you to respond to him. But how do we respond to God's love? Before we talk about this, I want to look at some of the crazy things that we believe we should do to respond to his love.

Earn it by doing good deeds

God created people with a purpose in mind: to have a relationship with each of us. All of us have made mistakes and done things that are wrong. These things are what God calls "sins", *and* we are separated from him because of them. Many people have the idea that they can make up for their sin, or bad deeds, by doing good deeds.

Have you ever seen a balance scale? It has two plates on either side, suspended by chains. They are balanced on a rod in the middle that is connected to a base. If you put items on one plate and other items on the other plate, the one with the most weight will hang the lowest. You can immediately notice which one weighs more, by seeing which one drops down the furthest. A lot of people think this is what God does with our sins on judgment day. We believe that he will take our good deeds to put them on one side, then our bad deeds to add on the other side. Whichever side has the most determines if we are good or bad and where we will spend eternity. Some think that God not only does this when we die, but that he does it regularly while we are alive to determine if he loves us or not.

If God is a good God, how could he love and bless someone who has done mostly bad things? Some people think the way to respond to God's love is by being good. This approach makes his love something we earn. We work for it by doing good things, which balances our scale, and then God will love and accept us. This sounds reasonable, right? Wrong.

I must change first

Another crazy thought that we have about God and about how to respond to his love is that we must change before we can respond. We think that, in order to get God to love us, we have to be good. Some even think they have to clean up their act and eliminate their bad attitudes, behaviors or habits. As a pastor, people have told me, "I know I need God, but before I turn to him I have to work on a few things in my life." You know you do things that God would not approve, so you think you have to stop doing them, right? Wrong.

Compare yourself with others

One more crazy idea that some people have about God is that he is weighing and comparing them with others. You may have messed up and done wrong things, but you rationalize that what you have done is not as bad as someone else's. You have told a few white lies, had lustful thoughts, even lost your temper and yelled at your friends; but you are not a bad person because at least you are not a murderer, thief or child molester, right? Wrong again.

Sin is sin. In God's eyes, it is all the same. It is rebellion against God's way, his righteousness. There are no big or little sins: if you sin, you are a sinner. We are all in the same boat. The amazing thing about God and his love is that he accepts you just as you are. You do not have to make amends or pay for all the bad things you have ever done. You do not even have to change your behaviors before you come to God.

You cannot earn God's love; it is unconditional and freely offered to everyone, no matter how bad that person is. The concept of unconditional love is difficult for most of us, because we have never experienced it before. We have been loved based on our performance, based on how we act or treat others, based on our looks, strengths and abilities. God loves and accepts you, just as you are. All you have to do is respond. How do we do that? It's as easy as ABC.

A - Admit you cannot save yourself

God knows we cannot save ourselves and solve our sin problem on our own. He also knows that sin separates us from him and keeps us from having the relationship with him that we were designed for. In his great love for us, he provided a way for us to know him: he became one of us.

God, our creator, became a man. His name is Jesus. "The Word became flesh and made his dwelling among us. We have seen his glory, the glory of the one and only Son, who came from the Father, full of grace and truth" (John 1:14, NIV). Jesus came to reveal the truth about God, as well as to provide us a way to be forgiven of our sin and to have a relationship with God. The way he did this is with Jesus becoming our substitute. Not only does our sin separate us from God, it also condemns us to death.

Consider this verse: "For the wages of sin is death, but the gift of God is eternal life in Christ Jesus our Lord" (Romans 6:23 NIV). In the Bible, God describes "sin" as breaking his law. The punishment for this crime is death. God does not want to punish anyone, but he is righteous and just and cannot look the other way at our sin. So he took upon himself the punishment for our sin by placing it on Jesus. Jesus, who never sinned, died in our place. Imagine if you were convicted of murder

114

and condemned to die by lethal injection. Just as they place you on the gurney to execute you, the judge who sentenced you comes in and tells the guards to kill him instead. So they strap and execute him, and let you go free. This is exactly what happened when Jesus died on the cross for you and me; God placed on him the punishment for our sin. He died for our sins as a perfect sacrifice, and now we can be forgiven. Finally, to prove that his death accomplished all of this, Jesus rose from the dead. Impossible? Not for God. If you are a skeptic, I urge you to look at the evidence of the resurrection.

All you have to do is stop trying to save yourself by your good works or self-effort at changing your life. You have to admit you are a sinner and you cannot save yourself. When you do, you open yourself to God and to his power to save you.

B - Believe that Jesus paid the price

The result of Jesus taking our sins and dying in our place is forgiveness. God can now forgive us of our sin because of what Jesus did. I have been blessed with the privilege of traveling to over thirty different countries, and I have shared the message of God's love with people of various religions. Only in Christianity do we have the concept of forgiveness. We do not believe that God puts our good and bad deeds on a scale. We do not believe that we can earn a relationship with God by being good. What we do believe is that Jesus died the death we deserved and rose from the grave, so that we could be forgiven and able to have a relationship with God. God has washed away our sin through the blood of Jesus, and now sees us as clean before him. We just need to believe it.

Believing in something does not mean you will not have doubts. To believe means that you accept it as true and trustworthy. The way we verbalize this is by saying "thank you."

C - Call upon Jesus

If you believe you have sinned against a holy God, and he has made a way for you to be forgiven, how do you respond to God's love? How do you receive this gift of forgiveness? The C in our ABC's of responding to God's love stands for Call. To call for something means to simply ask for it. All you have to do is ask for God's forgiveness, which Jesus provided. In our church, we invite people to do it by saying a simple prayer that goes like this:

> *Dear Jesus, thank you for loving me. I admit that I am a sinner and ask you to forgive me of all my sin. Thank you, Lord, that you will forgive me because you died on the cross for me and rose again. I give you my life, and promise to put you first and live the way you want me to. I love you, Jesus. Thank you for loving me. Amen.*

How to grow in your connection with God

Just like a wedding vow is the beginning of a marriage, asking Jesus to forgive you is the beginning of your connection with him. If you want this connection to become strong, there are some practical things that you can do. These will help you grow in your relationship with him. You do not do these things to earn his love, but in response to it. In the same way you ask your spouse what you can do to show your love to him or her, we do these things out of a heart full of love and because they will bring us closer to God.

Read the Bible

One of the most important things you can do to strengthen your connection with God is to read the Bible. The Bible is not like any other book. I have read plenty of them, but there

Turn it up!

are only a few that I have read more than once —and once I have done that, I know pretty much what it says.

But the Bible is different. Every time you read it, you will see things that you never saw before. God will speak to you and encourage you. He will also remind you of how much he loves you and what plans he has for your life. We are not following a religion, we have a relationship with God; and, in any relationship, communication is critical. The primary way God speaks to us is through the Bible. It is His word to you, his love letter. Reading His word regularly will establish a strong connection between you and Him. You will grow stronger in your faith and you will love Him more, as you let Him speak to you from the Bible.

For some, the Bible can seem very intimidating at first, but do not let that keep you from reading it. You are not alone in this. God has left his Holy Spirit with us to teach us and help us understand. Just read it like any other book, let God speak to you through it. Reading it and talking about it as a couple will help you to strengthen your relationship with each other. I suggest you start by reading about Jesus in the books of Matthew, Mark, Luke and John.

Pray

Prayer is a key component to a strong connection with God. Prayer is simply talking to God just like you would talk to someone else. There are ways to pray and formulas that you can follow, but prayer is sharing your thoughts with God and then listening.

Sometimes, I like to write out my prayers to God. I also talk to him while I am walking or driving. I also like to use the Lord's Prayer as an outline for organizing my thoughts. I encourage you to pray as well, as an individual and as a couple, regularly. Holding hands with your spouse when you pray together is an extremely powerful thing to do. It will draw you closer to God and to each other. Jesus said: "Again, truly I tell you that if two of you on earth agree about anything they ask for, it will be done for them by my Father in heaven. For where two or three gather in my name, there am I with them" (Matthew 18:19-20 NIV). When you come together as a couple to pray, Jesus is there with you. You are uniting with each other and also with him. There is a great power when we agree in prayer with another person, especially with your spouse —the most important person in your life. It is very powerful when your prayer partner is also your life partner. When we agree in prayer, Jesus promises that our father in heaven will do what we ask Him to.

Prayer is also surrendering our plans and desires to God. When the disciples asked Jesus to teach them to pray, one of the items he told them to include was: "your kingdom come, your will be done, on earth as it is in heaven." (Matthew 6:10 NIV). God invites us to submit our lives and ask for his will to be done in each area of them.

Do not worry about the words or how to pray. It is not some kind of magic where you have to say things just right in order to get it to work. Just talk to God about the specific concerns of your life. As you pray together, you are inviting Him to be involved in your marriage and in your life.

What to pray for

What can you pray for as a couple? The answer is everything! "Do not be anxious about anything, but in every situation, by prayer and petition, with thanksgiving, present your requests to God" (Philippians 4:6 NIV). Everything that you go through in life can be and needs to be covered in prayer. Pray for your jobs, finances, relationships with friends and family, your kids, your health, your church and your community, literally everything.

Here are a few suggestions on what to ask God for when you pray:

Wisdom. Wisdom is knowing what to do in a specific situation. In your own personal times of prayer, ask for wisdom on how to be a great husband or wife. God will show you what to do when your relationship is challenged. He will give you creative ideas on how to show your spouse you love him or her. As a couple, pray for wisdom on how to manage your finances, how to raise your children and how to deal with other challenges of life.

Guidance. When faced with decisions, like buying a house or whether to take a job offer, ask God first. God knows what is best for you, so he will show you the right thing to do. If you follow his guidance, he will keep you from making mistakes and bring his blessing into your lives.

God's intervention. There are some problems you just cannot fix. Perhaps you have a co-worker who is maligning or gossiping about you. You have asked them to stop, but they will not. There seems to be nothing you can do about the problem. Ask God to fix it. He will do what is best when you relinquish the situation to him. He may give you the grace to cope with this coworker, to love him or her, and to pray for them. He could change your coworker's heart. He could also remove the problem. One day, you show up to work and find that this coworker, who you were struggling with, has been transferred to another department or moved for some other reason! I encourage you to ask God to resolve the things that you are powerless to change. He is a miracle working God.

Provision. Jesus taught us to pray for our daily bread in the Lord's Prayer in Matthew 6:11. God knows you need food, clothes, a place to live and transportation. He wants to be your provider.

God's favor. Favor is God doing something special for you. If you need a job, pray for favor. When that potential employer looks at your application, God will speak to them and tell that boss to give the job to you. They may say. "I do not know what it is about this person, but I feel the job needs to be theirs." That is favor. Favor also brings new opportunities to your life. You may meet the right person, the one who can open a door and make possible something that you never imagined. The saying is true: "It is not what you know, but who you know that counts." God can connect you with the ideal person to further your career, show you the perfect house, give you the best deal on a car and many other things.

God's blessing. Praying for a blessing is similar to praying for favor, though slightly different. Asking God to bless you is similar to asking him to make you successful in all your endeavors. Instead of failure, you will experience success. When God blesses your life, he puts his super on your natural, and you experience good things that you did not expect. When you are blessed, among other things, your refrigerator and car can last longer, you can be promoted at work, and you can have a great marriage. Regularly asking God to bless your connection invites him into your relationship and, in this way, he can put his power into your efforts.

Expect God to answer your prayers

When you pray, expect God to answer your prayers. The Bible calls this faith. Through life, I have learned that faith really comes down to what you expect to happen after you pray. The way to express this is by thanking God for what you have asked for even before you even receive it. When you ask God to heal you physically, thank him for doing this before feeling better. Thank him for giving you a great job, even if you are still looking. In this way, you are expressing your faith in the fact that He is your provider and that his answer is on its way.

Does this mean that life will be pain-free and problem-free? No. God never promised us that kind of life. What he does promise us, though, is to be with us in the middle of the storms in our lives. He promises us strength and wisdom to know what to do in challenging situations. Troubles will come in this life, but God will be with you and give you what you need to deal with each and every problem. Here is a promise to remember: "The righteous person may have many troubles, but the LORD delivers him from them all" (Psalm 34:19 NIV).

Follow the Bible

Even though you can pray for God's blessings, you can also experience them by doing what He tells us to do in his book. When you read the Bible, you will see that God gives us instructions on how to live, how to treat others and, most importantly, how to have a relationship with him. We obey God not just to avoid sinning, but because we can have better lives by following and obeying his directives. After all, he created life and knows how best to live it.

One way to think about this is to consider the Bible as the owner's manual to life. If I want to know how to change the clock on my car, I look at the manual that tells me how each part of my car works and how to adjust them. When you follow the instructions in your car's manual, it works better. In the same way, when we do what God tells us to do in the "owner's manual" of life, life works better.[16] We do not obey or follow the Bible to earn God's love or blessing, but when we do what he tells us to do his blessings come to us.

I love this verse: "The LORD will send a blessing on your barns and on everything you put your hand to. The LORD, your God, will bless you in the land he is giving you." (Deuteronomy 28:8 NIV). It doesn't matter if I am painting a room in our home, pulling weeds, mowing the lawn, talking to someone in my office at church, planning an outreach event, or whatever, I ask and expect God to bless what I am doing. When you obey God, you are letting yourself be blessed. He will make you successful in all you do.

Church

Another thing that is crucial to growing in your connection with God is attending a local church. In a church service, you experience the presence of God, which builds you up and strengthens your faith. You also receive the practical teaching of God's word and principles to live a successful life. Even more than that, you get the opportunity to give and bless others.

The life of faith is not to be lived alone. God wants us to connect with his people regularly. The relationships you build with God's people in a local church will be a source of strength and blessing to you, and you to them. We all need encouragement. In a local church, you can be that source of encouragement to others, and they can be the same for you. In your church, you can meet couples in great marriages and learn from them. You will also meet couples that you can mentor and encourage in their marriage. You do not have to be a pastor or church leader to minister to others, there will always be people who need what you can offer. You will be blessed and have a great marriage when you get plugged into a good local church.

Serve others

Another way that we grow closer to God and strengthen our relationship with him is by serving others. Here is what God promises us: "For we are God's handiwork, created in Christ Jesus to do good works, which God prepared in advance for us to do." (Ephesians 2:10 NIV). We do not do good works just to be saved or to earn God's love and blessing, but because we are saved.

Serving others can take many forms. It can be with an organized ministry at your church, such as working with children or youth. You could also be a greeter or usher, or be part of your church's ministry to the community. Consider starting a group that meets in your home and invite your neighbors. Some couples want to serve together, while others prefer to serve in different areas. If you do serve separately, be sure to share with each other what you both are experiencing. The important thing is to let God use you. His spirit and power will flow through and use you to make a difference in someone's life.

You can also serve the Lord by reaching out to family members and friends who do not know Jesus. Pray for them and ask God to give you natural opportunities to share his love. You do not need to preach or pressure them into believing; instead, serve and build your relationship with them by doing things together. As your friends and family see God working in your life, they will naturally ask you questions about your faith. Invite them to come to church with you, and watch how God will use you to impact their lives.

Listen to God's voice

One of the greatest blessings of having a connection with God is being able to hear his voice and to allow him to guide you. Prayer is not just about presenting a laundry list of requests: it is a two-way conversation between you and God. Expect him to speak to you. For the majority of time, his voice is something you can hear in your thoughts, not with your natural ears.

For me, God's voice is stronger and more persistent than any other thoughts I have. When He is telling me to do something, I hear or have that same thought over and over. The scripture says: "For those who are led by the Spirit of God, are the sons of God" (Romans 8:14 NIV). God wants to speak to you, and he will. All you have to do is identify those thoughts that come from him. Before the caller ID was even a part of our phones, you had no way of finding out who was calling you —at least not until you picked up the phone and they identified themselves. Once you heard their voice a few times, though, you usually learned to recognize it. Personally, I have heard Carrie's voice over the phone so many times by now that I have no problem recognizing it.

Give yourself permission to learn to recognize his voice. Try this: next time you get a thought that you believe might be God leading you to do something, do it. If it is immoral, illegal, or will hurt someone, then that is obviously not God. If it is not going to hurt you or anyone else, then obey and see what happens. For example, one day I was driving down the freeway when I had this sudden thought of stopping by a certain store, to check if they had a certain pair of shoes that I had been looking for. So I stopped and, sure enough, those same shoes were there on sale. The store even had my size. Now you may say that was coincidence, but I do believe that it was God guiding me so that he could bless me with a good pair of new shoes. When you obey these spontaneous promptings, you will notice that He will lead you to blessings. The more you do this, the easier it will be to recognize God's voice and to obey.

When you are learning to recognize the voice of God, look for the confirmation that will also come as part of his direction to you. He will open doors, or you will get the same input from other people. When you are making a big decision and you ask others for their input, the answer that you receive will confirm what God has been telling you. It is important to give yourself permission to get it wrong, though. You are not perfect and your ability to recognize God's voice is a work in progress. Sometimes you will get it right, other times you will be mistaken. Look for confirmation from circumstances, as well as from other people, before you make a big decision. Just know that God loves you, and that He wants to direct you to his best for your life and your marriage.

Your spouse will also confirm God's voice for you. Imagine that you and your spouse are taking turns praying about a certain problem. While your husband or wife is praying, a thought about what to do in that situation comes to you, and somehow this one seems a little different than all the other thoughts you had. It seems to have come from another source, different than your own mind. You think this might be God speaking to you, but you are not entirely sure. After your spouse stops praying, you tell them about the idea that just came to you. As soon as they hear it, they say: "Wow, I just had that same idea!" God will speak to both of you about the same thing. You are one as a married couple, and he will direct you as such. He is not going to say something to one of you and then something different to the other. He wants you to make decisions together, so listen to his voice and follow his guidance.

Not only will God guide you spontaneously to blessings or help you make the right decisions, but he will also speak to you about your relationship with your husband or wife. He might offer you a creative idea of something to do, like a gift to give or a note to write, to make your spouse feel special. He will also speak when you have done something to hurt your spouse. He will tell you to apologize, to ask for forgiveness, and he will also tell your spouse to do the same when they have hurt you. There will be times when God will speak to your spouse, to let him or her know they have done something wrong. You will not even have to confront them, since God will do it for you.

He has also prompted me to ask Carrie how she is doing. In those moments, I will sense that she is not okay, and that she needs me to listen and support her. When I obey these promptings, I see how God blesses our relationship. Carrie and I grow closer to each other because we do our best to listen and respond to God's voice.

Conclusion

You and your spouse can have a great marriage when you work regularly on turning up the connection you both share. However, it all starts by loving God and having a growing connection with him.

He really is the source of life and he wants to bless us in our marriages. How can he do so? By guiding, protecting, giving his strength to say no to temptation, and by showing you how to best love your spouse. As you grow in your relationship with God, you will see him bless your marriage, filling it with love.

The fifth commitment I encourage you to make is: *I commit to loving God and asking him to help us turn it up.*

With each other:

1. Do you think a connection with God is important in turning it up? If so, why?

2. Can you identify with any of the crazy ways people try to relate to God? The ones we looked at here are: earning God's love, changing yourself first and comparing yourself to others.

3. What concept in this chapter challenged you or spoke to you the most?

4. Several things were mentioned that we need to do in order to grow in our connection with God, such as going to church, praying, reading the Bible and serving others. Discuss which ones of these you would like to be more consistent in and develop a plan to get there.

PART THREE
FIVE SKILLS
TO LEARN

CHAPTER SEVEN

SKILL #1

SHARE YOUR FEELINGS

*I will share my feelings with you
and support you when you share yours.*

If you want to have a great marriage, you need to regularly turn up the intensity of your connection with each other. In addition to the commitments you make in order to do this, you also need to learn some skills.

In the remaining chapters, I will teach you five skills that will strengthen your marriage. Remember that a skill is different from a commitment. Generally, it is something that you learn how to do, so you can later use in a specific situation. The first skill that I will teach you is crucial to the health and strength of your marriage; and I assure that everyone can do it. If you want to turn it up and have a great marriage, you have to share your feelings. *"I will share my feelings with you and support you when you share yours"*.

Each of us is a complicated collection of experiences. Things happen to every single one of us, all day long. For example, you wake up in the morning, get ready and go to work. Typically, most of us do not spend the day with our spouse; we go our separate ways, only to reunite again in the evening. Situations occur around you and to you throughout the day. You participate in activities that may be enjoyable and/or challenging. You read things or watch something on television that impacts you. You may have a long commute and spend time talking over the phone, or listening to music, podcasts, audio books or the radio.

My point is that what you do all day can touch, inspire, influence or, in some way, affect you, in both significant and insignificant ways. Some of these events or experiences can be life changing, others are just normal everyday occurrences. Likewise, your spouse is having similar experiences. But neither of you will ever have an idea of what the other is going through, unless you start articulating these things to one another. You need to share more than just what happened. To grow closer, you need to share what you feel about everything that occurs in your life on a daily basis.

Three levels of communication

One of the essential ways to consistently turn it up, so you can have a strong connection and a great marriage, is to share your personal experiences with your spouse regularly and in detail. Seems pretty straightforward and easy to do, right? In fact, this seems so obvious. Why is it even in this book?

Of course, when you love someone, you are naturally going to tell them about all that happened through your day. Unfortunately, some couples do not know how to share these thoughts or feelings with each other. They may talk about their daily events or happenings, but never share what they think of these experiences or the impact they may have on them personally. One or both partners may lack confidence or skills to effectively communicate on a deeper level; remember, however, that this is essential for your connection.

There are three levels of communication. The first level is the event level: you tell your love about what happened that day. Most of us are pretty good at sharing this level of information. Over dinner or when you first get home, someone asks: "How was your day?" So we share things like: "There was an accident on the freeway; the boss told me that Johnson is leaving; I got a new assignment; I heard that Congress is considering raising our taxes; The Dodgers traded their star pitcher." This is the surface or external level.

The next level is thoughts. Here you share what you think about what happened. "I wonder why Johnson is leaving; I wonder if there might be a problem in my company; I bet the boss is going to give me his work." At this level, you may analyze or evaluate the event.

The third and deepest level is the feeling level. This is where you share what you feel, your emotions and reactions to what you have heard or experienced. "I feel frustrated and unappreciated at work. Johnson is leaving and I am afraid that the boss is going to dump all his work on me. Do they not know how hard I am working already? What if I cannot keep up with all that I am asked to do? I am worried that I might lose my job, if that happens how will we pay our bills?"

Can you see the difference in these three levels of communication? [17]

It's hard to share feelings

Unfortunately, sharing your feelings can be challenging. I cannot tell you how many times I have listened to frustrated wives, whose husbands never share their feelings with them. They long to be closer, but there seems to be a wall that keeps them apart. Even though this is something that many men identify with, women can struggle with sharing their feelings as well. Couples that have achieved great marriages not only have learned how to share what happens in their lives: they have also learned how to express what they think and, more importantly, how they feel. They have learned to share their hearts with each other. There are several reasons why it is difficult to share your feelings, and here are some of those reasons.

It's not the right time

Sharing your feelings is not complicated, but it does take the effort to learn the necessary skills to do so. Sometimes it is all in the timing. How do you feel when you get home from work? For many of us, the answer is simple: tired. You may be physically exhausted from a long day at work, and you do not want to talk when you get back home. You do not want to be rude and you wish to connect with your spouse, so you share some of the important points. Your conversation basically stays at the event level. It is not that you do not want to share at the feeling level, you just may not have the energy at the moment. You say to yourself: "I really want to share what I think and feel about this, but I am too tired right now. I will do it later." The problem is that, in our busy lives, later never comes.

It's too difficult to talk about

In some professions, such as police officers, firefighters, ambulance workers, nurses, and other first responders, it is necessary to keep thoughts and feelings at bay to get the job done in the most efficient manner. If they keep their feelings to themselves, these men and women often develop problems

—including Post Traumatic Stress Disorder (PTSD)—because they are not able to articulate the effects of all they see, hear and do on their jobs. In my service as a police chaplain, I have seen this devastation first hand. Imagine you are a police officer and are required to respond to a call where a seven-year-old has accidentally shot his little brother with their dad's handgun. What if you had to shoot someone or, worse yet, one of your fellow officers is hurt or killed?

I once heard a fireman tell the story of how he responded to a car accident, where a truck had flipped over and pinned the two occupants underneath. He and his team were unable to lift the truck: if they lifted one side to free one of the victims, the other would be crushed. They had to wait for special equipment to lift the truck straight up. While waiting for help, he sat and talked to one of the victims, a boy about the same age as his own son. He watched this young man slowly die from his injuries. Even though they were able to save the other victim, the death of the boy he comforted and reassured will haunt him for the rest of his life. How do you talk about something like that when you get home from work? You may talk about what happened, but just on the surface level. The terrible things that one sees, hears and experiences may seem just too painful to talk about, so you say to yourself: "I will deal with this later." But once again, later never comes, the experiences are not processed, and the feelings are stuffed inside. When your spouse asks how you are doing, you just say: "I am ok."

Most of us do not deal with traumatic injury, violence or death as a regular part of our day. Other things, however, can trigger responses in us because of past experiences. Perhaps someone at work tells you about someone being abused as a child, which elicits memories and emotions from your own childhood. This can provoke feelings that seem too painful to bear. When your spouse asks you about your day, you may not even mention this experience, and certainly not your response to it, because it is just too hurtful.

It's hard for my personality type

Sometimes sharing our thoughts and feelings is just not a component of our personality. One of the most amusing things that I see in premarital counseling is when one person is an extrovert, naturally open and talkative, while the other is an introvert, very reserved and quiet. In some couples, the difference is so extreme that you wonder how they are attracted to each other.

Talking energizes extroverts. They come home from a hard day and, even though they are exhausted, they talk. It is like a jolt of caffeine. On the other hand, talking usually drains introverts. If you are an introvert, it can be challenging to talk when you are tired, while sharing your feelings is even more difficult. If you want to have a great connection with your spouse, sharing your feelings is well worth the effort.

I do not know how

Sometimes we have trouble sharing our feelings because we just do not know how. Maybe you were never encouraged to share them as a child, so you never learned the vocabulary your spouse seems to know well. Perhaps you got into trouble when you tried to express strong emotions, especially the ones considered negative, like anger, frustration or fear. You were told to keep them to yourself, so you learned to bury or deny feelings that were uncomfortable for you or others.

Now, you are in a relationship where your spouse wants to be a part of your life. They want to hear about the events you encounter and how they make you feel. They want to help you process your thoughts and feelings, as well as to share their own. If either of you are ill equipped, this will present obstacles that both of you need to overcome. Because you never were encouraged to share your feelings while growing up, you just do not know how to identify them, let alone to put what you are feeling into words. Perhaps you are in a funky mood, but you are not sure why; so when your spouse asks you about this, your honest response is: "I do not know."

Do not give up

Because of these obstacles, many spouses and couples are tempted to give up. It is hard and sometimes painful to share your feelings. It is easier to just talk about the events than to share how you feel about them. However, when you do not share your feelings with your spouse, the quality of your connection will be limited and shallow. You may have a marriage that looks good on the outside, but that is not fulfilling to either of you on the inside.

You can learn to communicate more effectively. When you are able to identify your feelings and to put them into words, you can connect on a deeper level in all of your relationships, especially with your spouse. When troubles hit your marriage, as they surely will, knowing how to share your feelings with each other will strengthen and deepen the bond that holds you together. When you lose a loved one, get sick, lose a job, or suffer some other type of crisis, your bond can save you and your marriage.

Here are some steps on how to share your feelings.

Decide to share

Be brave and be willing to share your feelings with your spouse. The first step is to decide to go there, which can be very scary. You may feel awkward or afraid because this is uncharted territory, but the risks are worth it. The burdens you share not only will seem lighter afterwards, but they will inevitably draw you closer to each other.

Use open ended questions

If you want to help your spouse share their feelings, think about the questions you ask. Sometimes the questions you ask fail to spark a conversation because you use closed ended questions. A closed ended question is anything that can be answered with just one word. For example, a "How are you?" can be answered with a simple "Okay"; and asking a teenager how their day at school was can get you a simple "Fine". So instead of closed ended questions, ask open ended questions. Instead of "How was work?", you could say "Tell me about your day." If you go see a movie, you could ask "What do you think of the movie?", instead of "Did you like the movie?" If your spouse is not very talkative by nature, asking open ended questions will allow you to have better and more significant conversations that will lead to a mutual sharing of your feelings.

Encourage sharing by using magic words

Even though I do not believe in magic, there are in fact a few magical phrases that you or your spouse can use to step into the place where you share your feelings. These phrases will open the door to sharing, just like saying "Open Sesame." The first one is: "Let me tell you how I feel." A variation of that is: "Let me tell you how this (event, experience, word, reaction) made me feel." When you say these two things, you are making a request. You are asking permission to be open and vulnerable with your spouse. You are asking your spouse to be supportive, as you attempt to put into words what is going on in your heart. Think of this as a doorway or gateway to something better. You are announcing that you are moving from the rooms of events and thoughts to the room of feelings.

When your husband or wife tells you about something that happened through the day, you can encourage them into going to the feeling level by using these magic words: "How did that make you feel?" This question invites them to explore reactions that they may have suppressed in order to survive. Another set of magic words is: "Tell me more." If your spouse gets stuck and cannot seem to explain their feelings, you can also offer a few suggestions like: "Did that make you angry, sad, frustrated or happy?"

As I mentioned before, if you or your spouse were not equipped with the tools to share your feelings as children, you may need to learn some vocabulary and communication skills. In Appendix A, I have included a list of feeling words that will help you learn the necessary vocabulary to describe your emotions.

Be sensitive and supportive

If your spouse uses any of these magic words with you, agree to go there with them. Your response during this very vulnerable time will either allow your connection to move to a new level of closeness, or cause your spouse to retreat to a place of safety. Unfortunately, this safety will produce a weak connection, not a strong one. If your spouse is sharing their feelings, your role is to seek to understand and give them freedom to express. Do not judge, correct or invalidate the feelings that are being shared. When your spouse looks at things differently, you will be tempted to correct their perspective. However, by judging their feelings, you will shut your spouse down and they will stop sharing. Their perspective may be inaccurate, based on faulty information or stemming from past experiences, but your job is to still listen and understand. In the next chapter, we will talk about how to understand and show someone that you "get it".

Be sensitive to the timing and the readiness of your spouse to share their feelings. I have found that there is a numbness that comes over people right after the death of someone they loved. It is an emotional version of shock. When you go into physical shock, your body shuts down certain things in order to keep the most vital ones going. Emotional shock is like that too: the person may not feel the impact of their loss until the shock wears off. So, trying to get your spouse to talk about their feelings during that period is usually not the best thing to do. Realize that he or she will need to process the event or loss, and at some point they will need to express their feelings. So create a time to revisit the event, bring it up casually when you are eating dinner or going for a walk together. Ask how they are doing. Ask them to tell you how they are feeling about what happened. God's word says; "Carry each other's burdens, and in this way you will fulfill the law of Christ" (Galatians 6:2 NIV). This means that we are to help other people carry their struggles and challenges, especially our spouses. This does not mean that we do it for them, but with them.

Sharing your feelings with your spouse allows them to enter your world, to know what you are going through and dealing with. You are not asking them for advice, nor are you asking them to fix the problem, but simply expressing your thoughts and feelings, thus unloading the burden. The time will come when you may want and need their input, but sometimes you just need to process something. This is extremely healthy emotionally and we all need someone to do this with.

Share, do not tell

Notice I have been using the word "sharing" throughout this chapter. I could have used a different one, like "tell", "inform" or even "talk about". These are all ways to describe what I am encouraging you to do, but I really like the image that comes to mind with the word "share".

In kindergarten, we are taught to share our toys. When you share, you take what is yours and you allow someone else to enjoy it or participate with you. When you share your feelings, you are doing just the same: you are inviting someone else to participate with you in your inner world. If you want to turn it up so that you can have a great connection with your spouse, it is not enough to stay on the superficial level. You must go deeper with each other and share your feelings.

Conclusion

Do you want to turn it up, and have a great marriage? You can by sharing your feelings with each other. You really can have a great marriage and a strong connection when you do this. You may think "I cannot do that", or "I do not know how." However, you can learn how to open up and share. While you face the challenge of learning how to share your feelings, you will notice that it will greatly enhance the connection you have with each other. It has been said that feelings are the windows of your soul. Well, sharing your feelings is sharing your heart. You will be glad to have made the effort to learn this skill.

With each other:

1. Several reasons were given as to why it is hard to share your feelings. Those are: a) It is not the right time; b) Something is too difficult to talk about; c) It is not my personality type; d) I do not know how. Do any of these reasons describe why is it hard for you to share your feelings? Talk about what you can do to overcome these challenges.

2. Think about something that happened to you recently and how it made you feel. Use the list of feeling words in appendix A to find the words, then share them with each other.

3. Practice being a supportive listener by using the magic words: "How did that make you feel?" and "Tell me more."

CHAPTER EIGHT

SKILL #2

UNDERSTAND EACH OTHER

I will seek to understand you and show you that I do.

As you were reading the last chapter on sharing your feelings, if you are a wife, you may have thought: "Yeah, right. I will never get my husband to share his feelings. He just doesn't do that." Perhaps you try to talk to your spouse about their feelings and they just never want to go there. Well, you might not believe it, but you could be one of the reasons why your spouse never wants to talk about their feelings or why they keep repeating themselves. To keep things turned up in your marriage and have a strong connection with each other, you need to learn and master skill #2: *"I will seek to understand you and show you that I do."*

This skill has two parts. The first one is to listen and "get" what your spouse is saying to you. The second part is to then let him or her know that you understand. By learning to understand, you will be able to support each other through challenging situations and to resolve issues before they become conflicts.

Two types of conversations that need understanding

There are two types of conversations that you will have with your spouse. These will require you to understand, as well as to show that you understand what they are saying to you.

The first one is a confrontation. Confrontations usually happen when one of you is upset about something. During this type of conversation, anger, frustration and other emotions are already impacting what your spouse wants to say to you. The desire or goal of this conversation is that something changes. When your spouse is upset about something you did or said, they do not just want you to know about their anger; they want you to apologize and do things differently the next time.

Have you ever been in an argument with someone who keeps repeating herself? It seems like the more they repeat why they are angry at you, the more heated the argument gets. Why do you think someone feels the need to do that? Well, it is usually because they do not feel like you understand them. They continue to repeat themselves to let you know how they feel, hoping that you will understand. One of the most common comments I get when talking to a couple where the wife is upset with her husband is: "He just doesn't get it." No matter how many times she tells him what she needs or wants, he just does not seem to understand and that makes her angry and frustrated. When an angry person feels that you understand the depth of their anger, they usually stop confronting you and then you can discuss what needs to be changed in order to resolve the issue or fix the problem.

The second type of conversation that needs you to show understanding is when your spouse is upset or struggling over something that happened to him or her. Let's call this type of conversation "sharing". Something happened and your spouse is struggling with it. The goal of this type of conversation is support: they do not need you to fix the problem, they just need you to support them in dealing with the issue. They are not mad at you. This conversation has nothing to do with something you did. But if you fail to give them your support, they may get angry at you and your connection will certainly suffer. Bad things happen in life, and one key part of being in a relationship is being there to support and encourage each other. Showing that you understand is key to turning it up, strengthening your connection and having a great marriage.

Understanding is challenging because we do not really listen

Let me assure you that this may seem like a challenging skill to learn, but you can do it. Before we look at how to understand your spouse, let's talk about why it is so hard for us to listen.

The first reason why it is hard for us to understand someone else's pain, anger or frustration is because, instead of listening, we focus on what we are going to say. Understanding starts with listening. You will not be able to understand anyone or anything, including your spouse, if you cannot listen. We all struggle with listening because our natural reaction when hearing something is to analyze what to say in response. Sometimes we think about similar things that happened to us, or we start coming up with excuses or reasons for why we did what we did. As soon as we think of an excuse, we interrupt and explain our behavior, instead of listening and understanding the heart of what our spouse is trying to say. When you do this, you will find that you will most likely misinterpret and invalidate your spouse, which leads to greater anger, frustration and hurt.

Sometimes it is difficult to listen because the words you hear trigger an emotion inside of you. Your spouse's sadness, anger or pain may cause you to relive or, at least, remember an experience from your childhood that felt out of control and terrifying. Now, instead of focusing on the message being sent by your hurt or angry spouse, you are thinking of yourself. When this happens, it is very difficult to resist the temptation of interrupting your husband or wife to start talking about you and your feelings.

If you are having difficulties in paying attention to your spouse as he or she shares, or if you find yourself thinking how you will respond rather than focusing on your spouse's words, feelings and impressions, you need to ask yourself why is this the case. Attend to this because if your spouse does not feel listened and understood, challenges in the relationship will emerge. To have the connection you and your spouse want and need for a great marriage or relationship, I encourage you to listen with the goal of understanding, not responding. This may seem impossible, but you can do this.

Understanding is challenging because we respond with judgment

Another reason why it is challenging to understand is because we tend to evaluate what we hear and then respond with words of judgment. We are looking to see if the statement we just heard is wrong, incorrect or simply inappropriate. When you tell your spouse what you think of what they just said, you are responding with words of judgment. You have put yourself in the place of a judge, rather than in the place of a caring husband or wife.

Sharing feelings can be difficult for multiple reasons, as stated in the previous chapter. if you experienced judgment when you tried sharing your feelings as a child, you may expect your husband or wife to treat you the same way. If you pass judgment when someone shares their feelings, they may pull back from you and stop sharing because they no longer feel safe.

Here are some examples of responses that are judgmental:

"Do not feel that way." This response tells your spouse that their feelings are wrong, or that they are wrong for having them. Feelings are neutral, they are neither good nor bad, they just are. Feelings also come and go. They are based on reactions and responses that may have their roots in past experiences, so you cannot just make them go away when someone tells you to.

Another judgmental response is: "That is not true, I really do care about you." You have just called your spouse a liar. You think you are saying one thing, but in reality they are hearing another. It also sounds defensive because you may be unwilling to own your part in the issue. Likewise, the spiritual response to a feeling goes like this: "Do not be silly, of course God loves you." Again, you are minimizing your spouse's doubts about God's love rather than helping them explore the reasons for these doubts.

Here's one last example of a judgmental response: "I know, your boss is a jerk." Whenever you start a statement with "I know...", you are telling your spouse that you do not want to or need to hear something again, which completely shuts down the sharing. Instead of being supportive, you are being dismissive and uninterested.

Can you relate to saying or hearing things like this from your spouse? I think all of us can. Even if you and your spouse love and want to share your hearts with each other, our default setting is to often judge and correct whenever we hear something untrue or inaccurate. Unfortunately, when we react this way, our spouse may no longer be willing or able to share their feelings.

All of us have this challenge. When you listen, grasp fully what your spouse is saying and then let them know that you get it. Another writer in the Bible puts it this way: "My dear brothers and sisters, take note of this: everyone should be quick to listen, slow to speak and slow to become angry" (James 1:19 NIV).

Understanding is challenging because we let our filters get in the way

A third reason why understanding can be challenging is because we let our filters or our own interpretations of things get in the way. Each of us has a worldview or filter that interprets reality for us. In the previous chapter, I discussed the three levels of communication: events, thoughts and feelings.

Life happens. You engage in activities, interact with others, hear or read about things in the news, and all of this is processed through a filter of your knowledge and past experiences. As it all passes through this filter, you interpret what life is throwing at you. You create thoughts and form opinions on what is happening. You draw conclusions and understand reality based on your knowledge and experience. You have to make sense of all the input that comes into your life, and your filter allows you to respond and live without going crazy. Anthropologists call this filter a "worldview", as it basically is your understanding of how the world works and how to survive in it.

If you generally see the world as predictable, then you know that, if you do certain things, you will be getting certain outcomes. For example, your experience tells you that, if you go to work every day, at the end of the week your employer will give you a paycheck. Getting paid several days from now becomes predictable. You also know that, when you go to the store you can use that money to buy groceries. So you go to work confident, knowing that you will be able to eat today and tomorrow. You are not afraid of going hungry.

However, if you see life as unpredictable, then you may be plagued with doubts and uncertainty. If you do not believe you will be paid after working all week, you may demand payment at the end of the day or stop working for others altogether. If you do not have the money, you cannot buy food. If you cannot buy food at the store, you will not go there. You may form an alternative plan to ensure that your family is fed or you will expect hunger to be part of your life. If life is unpredictable, you live in a constant state of worry and fear, and you may always be on the lookout for ways to make your situation more secure. In another scenario, if a person has experienced a lot of failure, they may eventually see themselves as failures and come to believe that, no matter what they do, they will never succeed. This person sees himself or herself as doomed to failure; therefore, they never take risks. They give up on life and lose hope.

Our worldview extends into our relationships. For example, if your parents were inconsistent with their love for you, you may think that people cannot be trusted. You may have a "proceed-with-caution" attitude, or be guarded, because you are afraid of getting hurt. However, if you were raised in a sheltered and protective environment, you may view the world and the people around you as completely safe. You may trust others without suspicion and be completely vulnerable because, to you, the world is a safe place and everyone can be trusted. We tend to interpret others' behavior in the context of our own worldview rather than theirs, which is unfair and, most likely, inaccurate. I know that both of the above scenarios are simplistic and naïve, but the illustration is presented so that you examine the contrasts and contradictions of the worldviews that you and your spouse may bring into your relationship.

Let go of your perspective

To understand each other, we must let go of our own unique perspectives or worldview. Your perspective on life in general or on a specific situation is neither right or wrong, good or bad, but it is yours and it is real for you. While our individual perspective may be valid, and each of us has the right to our own point of view, it can also be a liability. Your perspective, often based on past experiences and prior knowledge, may not line up with the reality of your current situation.

When your spouse shares their feelings, they are also speaking from their perspective, from their point of view. They may have already created an interpretation of an event based on their filter. When you hear a perspective that does not sound true or that does not line up with your understanding of reality, you may immediately want to correct your spouse. The problem is that, by doing this, you invalidate your spouse's perspective and judge them. As I said previously, judgment usually shuts down any further communication. If you want to have a strong connection with someone, let go of your perspective for a moment and seek to validate their thoughts and feelings; this way, you can understand the interpretation and feelings behind what they are trying to say.

Learn to validate

People often come to me with their problems and crises. They may also share their interpretation of those challenges, based on their worldview, which may be incomplete or incorrect. For example, they may say: "I feel that God has abandoned me", or "I do not think God loves me." My natural instinct is to interrupt and correct them. Left to myself, I may say: "You're wrong! God does love you. Let me get my Bible and show you what it actually says." However, I have learned over the years that such a response just silences the person who has come to me for help. If I correct someone, I make them feel inadequate, ignorant and condemned. Instead of helping, I have only made it worse. While I may believe that their interpretation of the problem is wrong, before I can help them, they need to know I understand them. The way to do this is by validating their interpretation. When I validate a person who does not feel loved by God, I let them know that I get it. I let them know that what they feel is valid, true or real for them at that moment in time. I acknowledge that the feeling is real, even if it may not be true.[18]

A few years ago, as I was teaching this concept of validation to some of the leaders at the church, one of them made an important comment. His job at the time was to train the people who provide technical support for computer problems over the phone. I am sure that you have called someone like this at least once, when your computer, phone or other gadget was not working properly and you were very frustrated. Before these tech support people can fix someone's computer problem, they first need to communicate to the caller that they understand their pain and frustration. Without that assurance, the caller will continue to talk about their anger instead of allowing the support person to fix the issue. Only after acknowledging the feelings of the caller, can the issue be addressed and a solution provided.

This holds true in your relationship with your husband or wife. In order to have a great connection with your spouse, even if their interpretation of an event or conversation is not accurate from your perspective, they need to know that you understand what they feel and how they came to that point of view. It is only after your spouse feels understood by you that you can then share your perspective.

Look again at the example of the person who feels that God does not love them. When I give them the freedom and opportunity to express their feelings, and to explain why they think this is true, they feel validated. Usually, after validating their feelings, I am able to share a scripture or provide another way to look at the problem. Before I do this, I must understand their pain and communicate that to them. When your husband or wife is upset, or when they are angry about something you did or said, they need you to understand their frustration or anger. They need to be sure that you understand. When they know you get it, they are more open to hearing your response on how to deal with the situation.

How to validate

I will never forget an encounter I had with an angry lady at our church. I was standing outside in the parking lot when she drove in, got out of her car, slammed the door and walked right up to me. It did not take a lot of discernment to see that she was angry. She told me that her son had recently been in a car accident and ended up in the hospital. She had called the church and left a message asking for someone to visit him. She was upset because no one ever called her back, and no one went to see him. For some reason, I had never gotten the message. If I had known of her situation, I would have responded promptly; but I did not know. I was tempted to defend myself, and the church, for not responding: "How could I respond if I never got the message?"

In other words, I felt like blaming her for not sending us the message correctly. But then I remembered what I had learned about validation and understanding. Instead of responding with any kind of explanation or reason on why she did not get a call back, I said: "I am so sorry that this happened to you and your son. If that happened to me, I would be really angry too. If my son was in a car accident and ended up in the hospital, and I called my church and no one called me back or visited him, I would be very mad too." After I said this, I could see her anger dissipate. It was like watching the air go out of a balloon. She calmed down, and I asked her how her son was doing. She told me he was home and doing well. She did not need me to do anything more, she just wanted me to understand her pain and frustration. Of course, I still apologized and promised to look into why our system had failed. Because she knew I had heard and understood where she was coming from, she accepted my apology.

How to show you understand

How do you let your spouse know that you understand? Here are the steps to show understanding:

First, listen without interrupting. If you hear those dreaded words, "We need to talk," or if your spouse begins to share something frustrating or painful or upsetting, realize that what you are about to hear is not just an ordinary message. What you are going to receive is important to the person speaking. Remind yourself to focus and listen, let them fully express what they need to say. Interrupting with an excuse, correction, explanation, or even with a question, can break the flow of the other person's thoughts; so hold your tongue.

Do your best to show that you are listening by nodding your head, maintaining eye contact, and, most importantly, waiting to respond until they are done. Many times, we do not really listen to others, especially if we are feeling unjustly attacked. Resist the temptation of thinking what to say in response and how to defend yourself. Instead, put yourself in their shoes and imagine how you would feel if that same thing happened to you. Do your best to concentrate and focus on what they are saying, so that you can understand their perspective and how important the issue is to them.

Second, repeat back what you just heard. Take what you just heard and repeat it back to your spouse, in your own words and in a calm manner. This will assure your spouse that you really are listening and trying to understand what they were trying to communicate. Imagine that your spouse is upset because you have repeatedly come home late from work, without letting them know. Instead of responding with an explanation on how things that happen at work make you late, respond with something like this: "I hear you saying that you feel angry at me because I didn't let you know that I would be getting home late tonight. I can see how this might cause you to worry, as I may have gotten into an accident or something else could have happened. The dinner gets cold and makes you feel like I do not care about you." Can you see how this response is focused on your spouse's feelings and concerns? There are no explanations, excuses or defensiveness. You are not angry at them for bringing this to your attention, but you are validating their feelings and showing that you understand the concerns.

Third, ask for feedback. Asking "Is that right?" allows your spouse to correct you or give a deeper expression of their concerns. If they have more to say, let them continue, then repeat step two by repeating their concerns in your own words. Do this until they tell you: "Yes, that's it." Your priorities are to let your spouse fully express their emotions and concerns, understand what they are going through, then let your spouse know that you get it.

Fourthly, respond. After letting your spouse know that you understand their thoughts and feelings, you are ready to respond. Your response to the particular concern about being late could be an explanation of why. It could also be an apology, along with a promise to call whenever you are going to be late, so your spouse knows when you will arrive home.

Step five, let your spouse respond back to you. Give them the opportunity to give feedback on your response. Back and forth this goes; but instead of talking *to* each other, you are now talking *with* each other. Your goal is to understand, not to get your point across.

Step six, brainstorm a solution. Once each of you has expressed your concerns and feelings about a problem or offense, you can then talk about how to solve or avoid that issue in the future. In the case of not letting your spouse know you will be home late, some possible actions could be to plan your work better, so that you can let your spouse know that same morning if you will be working late. Another possible solution is to make a promise: if an emergency hits late in the day, you will call right away to let them know about it. The point is that you devise a plan of action, which will be implemented if something keeps you from being home at your usual time. When both of you agree to it, you can then breathe a sigh of relief. The plan has now been put in place. Of course, make sure to stick with the plan the next time you are late; or another heated conversation will certainly be in your future.[19]

Some problems do not require a solution

If your spouse is going through a difficult situation, remember: they want and need your support, but they may not want you to try to fix the situation. Just as validation does not require agreement, understanding does not always require you to fix or provide advice regarding the challenge.

People come to me almost every day with their problems. My job is to listen and understand, to give them Biblical input and wisdom regarding their situations, and to pray with them. A big part of my role as a pastor is to provide answers to their questions and possible solutions to their challenges. In other words, I try to fix what is wrong if possible. However, I have learned that this is not usually what my wife wants or needs from me when I arrive home. Instead, she wants me to understand and support her.

Unless your spouse specifically asks you for your input or to do something to change the situation, it is best to not provide a solution or give unsolicited advice. When my wife shares with me a problem or challenge she is facing, I have to remind myself not to go into fix-it mode, but to use the understanding skill to let her know that I get it and I support her. I listen and respond by putting her thoughts and feelings into my own words. I seek to simply understand. There have been times when I have done this and later she has asked: "What do you think I should do?" At that point, she wants my advice. Until she asks for it, though, I try to remember to just be her husband, not her pastor or coach. This is challenging for me, so I often fail to show understanding in the way my wife needs me to. But sometimes I get it right, and you can do it also if you learn and practice this skill.

Why it is not always a question

In the same way that your spouse wants you to understand and not try to fix the problem, sometimes they may ask questions that do not have answers. One such question is: "Why did God let this happen?" When I hear someone ask this, I remind myself that they may not be looking for a theological answer on why God allows suffering in the world. That person is usually just venting their frustration and expressing their feelings about a situation. Their questions, feelings and expressions are not indicative of a lack of faith; instead, they are a cry to God, who understands more fully than I ever can. It is natural and understandable for someone in pain to ask "Where is God?". Dr. John Townsend writes:

> For many people who struggle, there is no real and true answer to the "Where is God?" question that will satisfy them. No explanation from a theological level, a spiritual level, a psychological level, or any level will make a difference to their current conditions. That is because many times, "Where is God?" is not actually a question they are willing to receive an answer to. It is a protest.[20]

When your husband or wife asks why something is happening, they are probably not looking for a well thought out reason or answer to a question: they are protesting. When situations in life cause pain, we protest or complain to express our dislike. It is our automatic response to injury, like saying "Ouch" when we fell off our bikes and skinned our knees as children. As adults, we protest by saying "Why?". Next time you hear someone say this, realize that they could be just expressing the fact that they do not like what is happening. The best thing to do is show understanding and support rather than trying to provide an answer.

Conclusion

Life really is full of problems and challenges. What you need is a husband or wife that understands what you are going through and is there to support you. If you need that, so does your spouse. To turn it up, strengthen your connection and have a great marriage, learn the skill of understanding. By using it, you can validate and support each other through the tough times in life. There will also be conversations where your spouse confronts you about something you did or said that upset them. When you focus on understanding, you can respond appropriately and resolve those issues. Understanding takes practice, focus and dedication, but you can do it.

If you find yourself in the middle of an argument, remember this skill and use it: *I will seek to understand you and show you that I do.* Your job, as a husband or wife, is to understand and validate the person to whom you made your wedding vows. Your spouse needs your support and encouragement as much as you need theirs. I have seen marriages fall apart because they never knew how to validate or understand each other, nor how to show if they did. You and your spouse are partners, which means you are in this together. You need each other. When the time comes —that moment when you or your spouse says "We need to talk"—, you will both know the best way to respond.

With each other:

1. Practice the skill of understanding by sharing a memory of something that happened to you while growing up. Express how it made you feel. Your spouse will then repeat it back to you in their own words and ask; "Is that it?" Continue to describe what happened and

how you felt. Then your spouse will repeat it back to you until you feel understood. Then switch places and allow your spouse to share their experience and feelings with you.

2. Talk about how this exercise makes you feel.

3. Validation does not require agreement with what is being shared, but simply understanding and communicating that what someone is experiencing is real for them at that time. Talk about situations at work, or with other family members, where you could have validated another person's experience.

4. What is your reaction to the phrases "Some problems do not require a solution" and "Why isn't always a question"? Discuss why it is important to be supportive of each other by understanding, not by trying to fix or solve a problem.

CHAPTER NINE

SKILL #3

ASK FOR WHAT YOU NEED

I will ask for what I need.

If you want to turn it up, have a great marriage and a strong connection, another key skill that you must learn is to ask for what you need. Unmet needs and unfulfilled expectations can damage and destroy your connection. It might be difficult to do this at times, but to have a strong connection that results in a great marriage, you need to master skill #3: *"I will ask for what I need"*.

Asking is hard because we want to be self-sufficient

Asking for what you need can be hard to do. One reason is because, deep down, most of us desire to be complete on our own. We do not like to be considered needy or dependent on anyone else.

This goes back to the Garden of Eden, when God created Adam and Eve. When the Devil tempted Eve to eat the forbidden fruit, he told her: "You will be like God" (Genesis 3:5 NIV). God is self-sufficient. He does not need us, but we desperately need him. The Devil was, in essence, tempting them to become self-sufficient. In other words, Adam and Eve would have been able to take care of themselves and not need God anymore. Of course, it was all a lie, so they learned the hard way that trying to be self- sufficient leads to death. God created us with needs, needs that are good. He wants to be in a relationship with us, and our needs connect us with Him. The same is true in relationships with others: our needs connect us to others and, even though we do not like to admit it, each of us has them. These needs drive us to reach out both to God and to people.

It is both good and desirable to be responsible and resourceful. However, we are made for relationship with God and others. This starts with the basics of food and water, and continues to things like love, respect, trust and even the need of being needed by someone else. There is no such thing as the self-made man or woman. We may think that we do not need others, but we do.

Even Jesus needed people. In his darkest hour, the night before he was crucified, he went to the garden called Gethsemane. He took three of his disciples with him and asked them to be there while he went to pray. He needed to share his anguish with someone, he needed his friends. In this same way, we need to admit that we have needs and reach out to others, in order to have those needs met.

Admit you have needs

Admitting your need is what Jesus meant when he said: "Blessed are the poor in spirit, for theirs is the kingdom of heaven" (Matthew 5:3 NIV). Being poor is to have lack or need. Being poor in spirit is not to be poor financially, but to be aware of your need for God and others.[21] When you admit you have needs, you can then connect with others who can meet them.

In chapter two, I said that the goal of marriage is to become one. That begins when you and your spouse make the commitment of living together and loving each other for the rest of your lives. Your union is for your mutual benefit because you are better together than you are alone. You will meet many of the needs of your spouse and he or she will meet yours. Admitting you have needs and allowing your spouse to meet those needs is another way to turn it up. Asking for what you need is the pathway of connection and intimacy, and it is essential to build a great connection that results in a great marriage. It is normal to need. In fact, you and your spouse will grow closer as you share and attempt to meet each other's needs.

Declare your dependency

The opposite of being self-sufficient or independent is to be dependent. Being dependent requires trust, which is the foundation of all good relationships and marriages.

As Americans, we cringe at the idea of being dependent. We even have a holiday to celebrate our independence! In marriage, we must be open and vulnerable about our needs. We need to trust each other in mutual ways, knowing that we are safe with each other. All of this can be scary at first, but as you grow closer in your marriage, experience love and acceptance, you will find that your trust will increase too.

I am not advocating being dependent in an unhealthy way or saying that you need to be helpless. There are things that you can and need to do for yourself. What I am suggesting is that you realize, by your own strength, that you cannot meet all of your own needs. You really do need God and you need people. Instead of going to the extreme of self-sufficiency or independence, or to the extreme of neediness or helplessness, strive to develop a healthy dependency. One where you allow yourself the freedom to have needs and the courage to ask for those needs to be met.

But how do we do that?

Your spouse is not a mind reader

According to another Biblical writer, James, "You do not have because you do not ask God" (James 4:2 NIV). Once again, God's word gives us wisdom so that we can have great marriages. If there is something you want and need, ask for it. If there is something that you lack and cannot produce on your own, ask for it. Though you may wish it, your spouse is not a mind reader. If there is something your spouse can give you and you don't have it and would like it, you need to ask for it.

The next time you are watching a romantic comedy on television or at the movies, notice how the source of the funny situation almost always comes down to one person assuming that their partner knows something that they do not. Someone can fall into the trap of: "If you love me, you should know what I want." That person makes assumptions and is sure that the other will deliver what he or she desires.

A great example of this is in the classic television show *I Love Lucy*. It seems like Lucy is always in a bind because she never wants to ask Ricky for something. She drops hints or tries to manipulate him into meeting her needs or giving her what she wants. Of course, misunderstanding occurs and the result is extremely entertaining. However, while it is amusing to watch others go through the antics of trying to get what they want without asking, it is frustrating and challenging to experience this in your marriage.

You may think that your spouse is not giving you what you need because they simply do not care. Not getting what you want or need results in feeling unloved. If this situation continues and all attempts to repair it fail, your marriage will be in deep trouble. In order to have a great marriage, let me suggest that you be responsive to the expressed needs and desires of each other. Your responsibility is to let the other person know what you want. Most spouses, if they are able, want to meet the needs and desires of the love of their life; but they cannot guess what is within your heart and mind if you do not relay that information to them.

In chapter one, for example, I told the story of how Carrie asked me to make her feel special. I am so glad that she decided to say something and ask for what she needed, instead of dropping hints. I was clueless to the fact that something was amiss, until she asked for what she needed. Once I knew something was missing, I was able to respond.

What do you need?

Before you make a request, it is very wise to spend some time reflecting and figuring out what you really want or need. It can be challenging to know exactly what your need is. If you seem to be unhappy at home, there may be something in your relationship that you would like to be different.

Identify what you would like to change and then think about how your spouse could meet that need or change the situation. Rather than blurting out that you are not happy, it is best to come to your spouse with a well thought out request. Take the time to think about what you want before you ask.

Make SMART requests

To let your spouse know what you want, let me suggest that you create SMART requests. SMART is an acronym that stands for:

S – specific

M – measurable

A – action oriented

R – reasonable

T – time oriented

Specific

Your requests need to be specific. If you want your spouse to be nicer to you, what does that look like? If you want flowers, ask for them.

Measurable

To let your spouse know what you want or need, it is very helpful to put a number on that request. For example, if you want them to take you out to dinner, let them know how often you would like to go. Perhaps once a week, or twice a month? If you simply ask to go out to dinner, your spouse could take you out once and later say that they met your request.

Action Oriented

When you make a request, it is also helpful to explain in what ways that request can be met. These action steps can give the other person ideas on how they can meet your need and make you happy. As I mentioned before, when Carrie told me she wasn't happy, she suggested I buy her "just because" gifts. This was a specific action oriented request that was very helpful to me. I now knew what I could do to make her feel special.

Reasonable

Ask yourself if your desire is reasonable. It is only reasonable if it is something that your spouse will be able to do, like asking them to change some behaviors. For example: "Please do not leave your shoes in the middle of the bedroom. Please put them in the closet or somewhere where I will not trip over them."

It would be unreasonable to ask your spouse to purchase something that your budget does not afford. It is also unreasonable to ask them to change their personality or adopt your preferences. For example, if your spouse is quiet and reserved, and you ask them to do something that demands them to be social and outgoing, this may be beyond their ability. Encouraging someone to grow by doing something outside their comfort zone is acceptable, but realize that you cannot change a leopard's spots, nor can you change your spouse's personality. Make sure your request is reasonable before you ask.

Time-Oriented

Finally, a SMART request has a time orientation. Adding a time element or deadline to a request changes it from a wish to an actionable item that is completed by a specific time. For example, "This weekend would you please clean out the garage?" is a better request than "Please clean out the garage." Now your spouse knows when you want to have it completed and they can respond accordingly.[22]

Care enough to confront

Here is a saying that is worth remembering: "Do not complain about what you permit."[23] If there is something going on in your home or relationship that you do not like, take action and do something to change it. If that situation involves your spouse, making a request is usually the first step. But if you refuse to do anything to change the situation, then you are permitting it to occur.

The issue or concern might be minor and instead of confronting it, you could just accept it and let it go. If it is a major concern, however, you need to address it and work out a solution with your spouse. Fretting and complaining will not accomplish the real change that could be good for your connection.

If you are afraid of making a request or bringing up a concern with your spouse, you need to ask yourself some questions: "Why am I afraid of confrontation? Why am I reluctant to bring up an issue? Why is asking for something so uncomfortable for me? Am I trying to be sensitive so that my spouse will not feel judged?"

Talking about these questions and your answers with someone —your spouse, a trusted friend, a coach or even a therapist— could be very helpful. Once you have reflected on why you are reluctant, work on this with your spouse and together address the issue. This can create an environment where you feel free to ask for what you need and free to bring up issues of concern.

How to make a request

Once you are clear on what you want and have created a SMART request, you need to communicate this to your spouse. Here are some things to keep in mind when you do make your request.

It always helps to start on a positive note with a compliment, acknowledging something that your husband or wife does that you appreciate, or reminding your spouse that you love and want to be close them.[24] If you want to request your husband to call home when he is going to be late, start by acknowledging and thanking him for working so hard for you and your family. This affirmation will take down defensiveness and start the conversation in a constructive way. If you just blurt out your request, your spouse could easily think that they can never please you or that you are just complaining. All of us hear a critical voice inside our heads at times that says: "You cannot do anything right." Instead of adding to a negative message that could already be bouncing around in your spouse's head, let them know that you love, believe in, and appreciate them. Be just as specific about why you appreciate them as you are about what you want.

After you have started the conversation in a positive way, you need to present your request clearly and with the time you would like to have it completed by. Start by talking about how you want to improve your relationship and be closer. If your life is busy that you are concerned you're not spending enough time with each other, you could request a weekly date night. Make that request by talking about how scheduling a date night, at least once a week, will build and strengthen your connection. Talking about the outcome you want to see will allow your request to be seen as the means to that end, rather than another thing your spouse has to do.

Allow your spouse to respond

After affirming your spouse, making your request and talking about how a specific action will strengthen your relationship, allow them to respond. There are three ways to respond when someone asks you to do something: "You can say, 'yes,' 'no,' or you can make a counter offer."[25]

Your spouse may agree with your request from the start, willing to do what you have proposed without question, but there is also a chance that they are unable to meet your need. The most likely scenario, however, is that a counter offer may be suggested and discussed.

A counter offer can include an adjustment in the time frame, breadth of the action, a compromise, or an altogether different suggestion to meet both your needs. If you ask your husband to mow the lawn on Saturday and he responds that he will do it on Sunday, he is making a counter offer. He is agreeing to do what you asked, but changing the time frame. Or if he responds by saying that he can mow the front lawn on Saturday, but not the back lawn, he is limiting the size of the task. If he suggests hiring a gardener, then he is proposing a different solution than the one you thought would meet your need. I realize that some of the things you ask for will not be as cut and dried as this, but I hope you see how this works. Remember you are making a request, not a demand, and you are giving your spouse the freedom to say "yes" or "no".

Be sure to get a response when you make a request. Many couples have significant arguments because, when a request is made, the person who presented the request did not wait for a response. They just assumed that their spouse would comply, simply because they asked. When they do not get what they want, they get mad. Allow your spouse a moment to either agree, decline or make a counter offer. Their response to you is a promise: by agreeing to your request, they are promising to do something by the time you agreed upon.

If you are the one receiving the request and you agreed to do something, make your word your bond. Realize you just made a promise and do you best to keep it. If you cannot fulfill the request by the time you agreed to, go back to your spouse and renegotiate the agreement. Ask for more time or ask to have the size of the task changed.

What if they do not do what they promised?

I bet I know what you are thinking as you read this. You are asking yourself: "What do I do if my spouse agrees to do something by a certain time, but they don't do it?" Depending on the complexity of the task or the request, it may be helpful to follow up on it by asking for a progress report before the due date.

For example, at her job, my wife can set aside money in a health savings account before taxes. Since I manage our finances at home, she recently asked me to add up how much we spent on healthcare last year, so we would know how much to put into this account. While this is not a huge task, it does take some time. If I agreed to have that answer by Saturday, she could ask for an update on Thursday as to my progress in fulfilling her request. She does not have to nag me, but she can give me a gentle reminder so that I keep to the agreed upon schedule. If I promised to have the task completed by Saturday, and that day is going to be a busy one with various activities, I do not want to wait until Saturday evening to start the task. Asking for, or giving, a progress report helps clarify the request and communicates the expectation that the task will be done by the agreed deadline.

If Saturday arrives and I did not deliver as promised, my wife needs to ask me why this happened. My wife needs to be able to count on me to do as I say. She may ask me: "Why weren't you able to do what you promised? Will you be responsible and follow through on other commitments you have made to me? Can I trust you to do what you have promised me?" Even though it may sound harsh, holding someone accountable for not fulfilling a promise they made to you is essential in successful relationships.[26] I realize this may be uncomfortable, but it is absolutely necessary. Your spouse may be a responsible person, generally able to complete tasks and fulfill promises, but may have had a difficult week. Having this conversation is usually all it will take to get him or her to fulfill what they committed to do.

After confronting me for not completing the task, it is important for Carrie to ask when will I complete it, so that a decision can be made in a timely manner. On a positive note, she could remind me how important this information is and how setting up this account could really help us financially. She could also offer to help or support me with the task. Perhaps, the reason that I was unsuccessful is because I needed assistance. Instead of getting angry at your spouse when they are unable to complete a task, ask them how you might help with it.

Reasons why we fail to complete requests

Unless your spouse is struggling with a mental or physical illness that limits their abilities, there are really only a few reasons why they may not have completed a request by a certain deadline. Here are a some of those reasons, along with ways you can empower your spouse to complete your request.

A lack of knowledge or skill. They may genuinely not know how to do what you have asked them to. You can either help by showing them how to do it or by finding the resources that will. For example, if you want your husband to replace a light fixture and he continues to procrastinate, maybe he lacks confidence in his abilities to perform this task. If you found an online video showing how to change a light fixture, you could watch it with him and encourage him to try.

A lack of time. Other items are taking priority over this task. Help by reprioritizing these other commitments or activities.

A lack of understanding the importance of the task. Your spouse may not see the urgency behind completing a task. You can help by explaining the importance of it, and how it will improve your lives and your relationship.

A lack of structure. Important things are sometimes not done because they are not written down or scheduled. In the busyness of life, things tend to get forgotten. You can help by creating a list of all the projects or tasks that need to be done and then helping your spouse set aside specific times to work on each project.

A lack of support. When what you have asked is a complex project, not just a simple task, your spouse may feel overwhelmed. There may be too many things for one person to do alone. You can help by offering to do part of the project yourself or by working on it together.

A lack of desire. Sometimes your spouse may not want to do what you have asked. We all have certain likes and dislikes, and perhaps what you have asked is just something they don't want to do. You can help by accepting this fact and then figuring out together an alternative to getting that need met.

A lack of being able to say no. The person receiving the request needs to feel the freedom to decline or counter offer. If they don't feel that it's ok to say no to you, or if they want to please you, they may overcommit. They may say yes and not have any intention of following through on that request. So they say yes, because they simply don't have the courage or strength to say no to your face. If this is the dynamic in your marriage, let your spouse know that you would much rather hear a "no" than a "yes" that isn't really coming from their heart. When they tell you they just don't want to do that task, you can then go elsewhere to get it done or do it yourself. Let the "pleaser" know that they are pleasing you by being honest and only committing to do the things they will really do.

Accept reality

My wife and I have friends who have been married for over forty years. They have a great marriage, but the wife very rarely cooks. The husband in this relationship could have requested that his wife changes her behavior, or he could have accepted her as she was. Years ago, he decided to accept the fact that she does not like to cook. At some point, he learned that this was not going to be something he could ever expect from his wife. Instead of making this a point of dissension, he figured out a way to solve the problem without ongoing conflict with his wife. They decided to eat out most of the time. Recently, she started cooking more often, but they either still eat out a lot or he cooks.

My point is the following one. After requesting something from your spouse, if you see that they are never going to be able to provide it, the best thing to do is to just accept that. Then figure out another way to have the need met. Include your spouse in the brainstorming of solutions, they have a perspective that you may need. This also applies to doing home projects. If your spouse is unable or unwilling to do home repairs, accept the reality of the situation instead of asking repeatedly, nagging or berating them. Set aside money in your budget and hire someone to do those things.

Do not be parental

Begging, nagging or pestering someone to do something is not part of a great marriage and certainly does not strengthen your connection. You are your spouse's husband or wife, not their parent.

Unfortunately, many wives treat their husband as one of the kids. If you ask how many children a woman has, some will even include their husband in the count. Their husband may constantly need someone to find their socks or car keys, cook their dinner and even clean up after them. They may be acting like children, but still expect to be treated like adults. This is not a mutual relationship or partnership. In a marriage like this, a husband wants his wife to act like his mom. The woman may be the responsible one in the family, managing the finances, cooking all the meals, doing the laundry. Of course, this results in a very tired wife and a disappointing relationship for both parties.

Sometimes, this scenario happens because one spouse is irresponsible and just wants to be taken care of. This dynamic can also occur when the wife or husband is controlling and unreasonable: they may desire to manage everything because they believe that things will only get done right when they do it themselves. The result is that he or she never lets other members of the family to contribute, and the spouse may become dependent on them to do everything. Taking a parental role with your spouse is unhealthy because it leads to anger, blame, and irresponsibility in your husband or wife.

Wives, your husband needs a spouse, not a mommy. He needs you to be his wife, he needs you to treat him like a responsible adult. Husbands, your wife needs a companion, not a daddy. All of us need to be treated like adults by our spouses and empowered to be responsible partners in the relationship. When you know what you want, make a request, discuss it and then create solutions with each other. By doing this, you are affirming your love and respect for each other. Remember that your spouse is an individual with their own way of doing things. They may think of ways in and through a difficulty that you could not have imagined.

So, if you want to have a great connection, give each other the freedom to grow and develop as individuals. If at every step your spouse is afraid to try something new, for fear of disappointing you if they fail, little growth will result. If you build a foundation of mutual love and respect in your marriage, there will be plenty of opportunities for you to grow into better people —better than you would be by yourself.

Brian Fikkert and Steve Corbett have written a great book called *When Helping Hurts*. It highlights how well-meaning individuals, churches and other organizations may actually harm those they consider poor and needy, instead of helping them. The same paternalistic attitude that poisons these relationships can contaminate your marriage and debilitate your spouse from being able to solve their own problems or develop into the person they want to be.

I spoke earlier about helping or supporting your spouse to fulfill a request, but it is critical to not take on a condescending or paternal attitude when you do so. If you see yourself as the expert, teacher or parent with your spouse, you position yourself above them. This prideful or superior attitude will produce resistance, not cooperation, and is not empowering to the other person. Instead, use every opportunity to work with your spouse. Do not lord it over them or do things for them. Supporting someone to fulfill a request needs to be a coming alongside and assisting, rather than a reaching down from a place of superiority or authority. It also means that you do not do things for them in an attempt to be helpful.

Corbett and Fikkert say: "Do not do things for people that they can do themselves".[27] If your spouse has trouble getting to work on time, see yourself as a friend that is there to support them in their efforts, not as their parent who nags or takes responsibility for getting them to work on time. If they experience fallout for their poor time management, do not rescue them. Though you may both suffer if they lose their job, you can be there to help them process what went wrong to prevent it from happening again.

Be grateful

It is also crucial that you remember to show gratitude when your spouse does what you asked them to, or if they come up with a creative solution to fulfill the request. Your reaction and response to their input is the key to mutual cooperation becoming a regular part of your relationship. If your spouse goes out of their way to do something you asked, to learn a new skill or to step out of their comfort zone, and you do not recognize that, you may discourage them from trying next time. Even if they do not get it quite right or do it the way you imagined, acknowledging their effort will empower them and build their confidence.

It is easy to think that a task that is always taken care of by your husband or wife does not deserve a thank you afterward. Even with repetitive tasks like cooking dinner, cleaning the bathrooms, doing the dishes, taking out the trash, paying the bills and mowing the lawn, it is important to affirm your appreciation to your spouse for helping the home run smoothly. If a task is demanding, difficult, or just plain dirty, it is equally important to acknowledge their effort and commitment to you and your family. One way to do this is by saying: "I know that was a difficult task and I just want to let you know I appreciate your hard work."

Consideration, gratitude and acknowledgment are fuel for your relationship and will help you turn it up so you can have a great marriage. All of us want to know that our efforts are appreciated. Showing gratitude is a way of saying "I love you", so be generous with your compliments, praise and thanks. Acknowledge your spouse for their contribution to your family and marriage. Do not assume that they know this because you said "I love and appreciate you" at an earlier time. Take the initiative and let them know often how you feel about them. No one gets tired of hearing the words "Thank you."

Conclusion

The way to turn up and maintain a strong connection with your spouse is to simply ask for what you want. It is helpful to think through your requests and then make SMART ones. After making your request, allow your spouse to respond by making a commitment and expect them to deliver on it. If your spouse does not do what they promised, talk about it and offer ways to support them.

Remember that your spouse is not a mind reader. Ask for what you want and need, and allow your requests and the meeting of those needs to turn up and strengthen your connection. Your marriage will be strengthened greatly when you *"ask for what you need."*

With each other:

1. Think about and share a situation from a relationship you saw on a television show or movie that could have been avoided if one party would have made a request.

2. Pick something fairly easy that you would like your spouse to do for you and make a request using the SMART format. Then allow your spouse to respond with a yes, no or counter offer.

3. Share your reaction to this quote from Brian Fikkert and Steve Corbett: "Do not do things for people that they can do themselves". What do you think this means? Are you guilty of being parental with each other? How can you empower without rescuing each other, while at the same time helping and serving one another?

CHAPTER TEN

SKILL #4

EXPRESS YOUR ANGER IN A
HEALTHY WAY AND FORGIVE

*I will express my anger in a healthy way
and give forgiveness generously*

Dr. Henry Cloud, a well-known Christian psychologist, tells the story about a marriage seminar that he was leading when he told all the couples to first think of the wonderful things they loved about their spouses. He said: "Think of the wonderful qualities you admire and that attracted you to that person. Let those feelings fill you." Then he had them turn to face each other and repeat these words: "Honey, I am a sinner. I will fail you and I will hurt you."[28] His point was that, though we love, we are still fallen broken humans and it is inevitable to hurt the ones we love. We do not intend to, but we often say or do things that sting, which we regret immediately.

This is why we need to learn the skill of expressing anger in a healthy way and giving forgiveness. Unfortunately, over the course of your marriage, you can almost guarantee that you will get angry at each other and then need to forgive. If you want to turn it up to have a great marriage and a strong connection, I invite you to learn and master Skill #4: *I will express my anger in a healthy way and give forgiveness generously.*

Anger is not bad

We need to realize that anger is not an emotion that is good nor bad, it just is. Many Christians think anger is bad because, in the heat of the moment, we say or do things that may be hurtful. If someone crashes into your car and then drives away without giving you their insurance information, for example, you have a right to be angry. Anger is a response to something that you do not like, a way to protest a situation.

Believe it or not, anger in a relationship can be a good thing. If someone you love does something hurtful, your angry response will tell them that their words or deeds are not okay with you. If that person loves you, they will seek to repair any damage they have done to your connection. Often, anger signals a violation of a personal boundary. Your spouse will realize that their actions caused you to be hurt and angry, which may even open a door to a deeper level of understanding and commitment in your marriage. It can be a catalyst for change.

Here's what God says about anger: "In your anger do not sin. Do not let the sun go down while you are still angry" (Ephesians 4:26 NIV). He does not say that anger is a sin, but not to sin when you are angry. What this means is that, in order to have a great connection, you will have to learn how to be angry at each other in a way that does not damage either of you or your marriage.

Two buckets

One of my favorite authors on the subject of leadership is John Maxwell. He teaches that everyone carries with them two buckets everywhere they go: one with water and one with gasoline. You can either put out the fire of another person's anger with water, or make it worse with gasoline.[29] This is true in all relationships. If your spouse is angry about something and you respond by getting angry back, the situation may escalate because your response is like gasoline. Responding with "I would be a better wife if you were a man who could keep a job!" is not going to diffuse your husband's anger; this will only make it worse. If your spouse is angry with you for something you did or said, do not defend yourself by blaming or making up excuses. Instead, pour water on the fire of their anger by doing your best to stay calm. Try to have a conversation that allows your spouse to tell you why they are angry and take the opportunity to apologize if needed.

In most cases, what an angry person really wants is to be understood. They want you to see how angry they are and why. As we talked about through previous chapters, if someone is angry, you should respond by listening, validating their feelings and letting them know you understand. You will be amazed at how your spouse's anger dissolves when you seek to comprehend instead of blaming, excusing or defending yourself. As the scripture says, "A gentle answer turns away wrath, but a harsh word stirs up anger" (Proverbs 15:1 NIV). Once you know how deeply you hurt someone you love and express that understanding, you can then apologize and ask forgiveness.

Anger is an emotion of grief

Anger is also one of the emotions of grief. Psychologist Elisabeth Kubler-Ross identified five stages of grief, with anger being the second one right after denial.[30] It is natural to be angry when you lose someone or something. If you lose your job, you will likely be angry about getting fired. If someone you love dies, it is natural to be angry with God and even with the person who has died. Expressing that anger in a healthy way is part of coming to terms with the loss. The goal of grief is acceptance of the loss.

Discover the real source

When you stop and think about why you are angry, you might discover that the problem is not really with your spouse. It is with another area of your life. If you are having major challenges at work, feeling powerless, overwhelmed or trapped, you may come home primed to get mad at your spouse for burning the dinner. Even though your spouse had nothing to do with you losing your job or the death of your father, you might have so much anger inside that it spills over at the slightest provocation.

If this happens, recognize what the real source of your anger is. It is not the little thing your spouse did wrong, it is the grief you are experiencing because of your loss. You do not say what you want to say at work, so you come home and kick your dog, yell at the kids or treat your spouse unkindly. If the situation does not warrant a forceful response, chances are that you are misdirecting your anger.

Ask yourself what you are really angry about. It just might be that you are projecting your anger about another situation onto your spouse. If that is the case, own it and talk about it with the one you love. Allow him or her to show you grace and to give you encouragement. Then, brainstorm together how to respond to the real source of your anger.

It is possible to express your anger in a healthy way that does not hurt the people you love. The first thing to do when you are angry is to separate the issue from the person who caused these feelings. Recognize that when you are angry, you may have been hurt. There is something going on that is unacceptable to you. Something happened that seems unjust or unfair. Maybe you were expecting your spouse to meet a need and they let you down; maybe your spouse said or did something thoughtless or cruel to you, so you responded with anger. The thing to realize is that, unless you are married to a psychopath who loves hurting people, it was probably not your spouse's intent. He or she does not want to upset you because they love you. Once again, you need to remind yourself that your spouse is not perfect and neither are you. It is critical that when you get angry at your spouse, you separate the issue from the person. In other words, you are angry because something was said or done; and that is the problem, not the person who did or said the thing that made you angry. Your feelings of anger are your emotional response to the hurt they caused. They made a mistake, they did something wrong, but the problem is their behavior, not who they are. Remind yourself regularly that you are married to someone who loves you. Your spouse does not want to hurt you, but they will make mistakes and so will you. By separating the offense from the person, you are addressing the behavior in a manner that fosters understanding, forgiveness and grace.

Do not generalize

When we get angry, we are tempted to generalize the source of the grievance and respond by focusing on the person, not on the issue or transgression. We do this by saying things like "You always" or "You never." These statements do not address the issue, but are generalizations to make your spouse the problem. When you generalize, you create a situation that leaves no room for reconciliation or repair. Another problem with saying "You never" or "You always" is that these statements are not true: no one always does the same thing.

Respond, do not react

Understanding that anger is an emotional response to an event also gives you the power to choose how to respond. You have the choice to respond to your angry feelings in a healthy and helpful way or in an unhealthy and unhelpful manner. You do not have to let your emotions take over; otherwise, you will regret it later. God has given you the gift of free will: you are not a computer or machine programed to respond in a certain way to a certain command. When you feel anger rising, recognize this and think about what is causing it to emerge. Decide to respond in a healthy manner that will allow you and your spouse to reach reconciliation.

In my work as a pastor, I have talked to many men who are not violent by nature, but who have let their anger get the best of them at least once. The stories go something like this. They reacted angrily to something their wife did or said. When their spouse responded in the same way, the situation escalated. The wife tried to leave, then the man tried to stop her by grabbing her arm. She pushed back and he hit her. She called the police. When the police arrived, she told them what he did. They have no choice but to arrest the man for domestic violence, even if the wife has now changed her mind and does not want him arrested. Unfortunately, the onus falls to the man, who made the choice to express his anger in an unhealthy way.

Avoid two extremes

When it comes to expressing your anger, there are two negative extremes. One extreme is denial, or to stuff it all inside. At some point, if you keep pushing down angry feelings, you will reach a breaking point where it all spills out onto whoever is nearby. You will say and do stuff that you will regret. So, instead of letting your anger escalate or build up, learn how to express without hurtful words or careless acts. Talk about things with your spouse after they occur. Be honest about your feelings, seek resolution, and then let them go.

The other extreme is to explode over every offense, no matter how small. Some people think that their anger always needs to be out in the open, regardless of how much damage it might cause. That does not mean you have the right to express it however you want. I encourage you to think about what you want and the best way to get it. Do you want a loving marriage where you are able to talk honestly about your feelings and needs? Do you want a relationship of trust and acceptance? Do you want a strong connection with your spouse? Exploding all over your spouse on a regular basis will not produce the good things that you want for your marriage. Own what you are feeling and try to identify the trigger for your response.

Talk about it

Anger needs to be expressed in healthy and productive ways. The best thing to do is to talk about it after you have calmed down. Own your response without blaming your husband or wife for your reaction. They may have done something that triggered your anger, but your emotional reaction is all yours. Focus on that and talk about it so that it does not contaminate your relationship. Use statements that express your feelings, such as "It makes me angry when you…" or "I am frustrated and angry now, can I tell you why?"

Allow your offender to apologize

Because your spouse loves you, when they hear that they have hurt or offended you, you can expect them to apologize. Letting your spouse know what they have done or said that made you angry will give them an opportunity to say "I am sorry." Now that they know what they have done, they also have the ability to do something different in the future. In other words, they get to repent. Repentance is not just being sorry for what you have done, it is also changing and going in another direction.

Make a request

After owning the fact that you are angry and seeking to understand what has triggered your response, you can make a request of your spouse. "Would you please do or say this next time?" or "Would you please not do that or say that?." Remember, as I said earlier, your spouse is not a mind reader. Give them a chance to modify their words and deeds, and to change course for the good of your connection. Give them grace after they have apologized. Let them know that you forgive them and accept the fact that they are not perfect.

Call a time out if needed

It is critical to set some ground rules for how to resolve conflicts. It is never appropriate to use physical force or intimidation when you are angry. Set that as a boundary that you will never cross, no matter how heated arguments get. Remember that listening and understanding usually deflate and dissipate anger; and what is needed for that to happen is one person responding in a calm manner.

But what happens when you both are angry at the same time? What if you both had a really bad day at work and end up yelling at each other at home that night? If this ever happens, call a time out. Before your anger gets out of control and either of you does something you will regret, stop and walk away from each other for an agreed period of time. Calling a time out is simply recognizing that you are both upset and need to cool down before the situation gets worse.

The best thing to do is to put the discussion on hold for a while, so that you can allow the emotional fire to die down. A timeout is not refusing to talk about the problem, but realizing that you are unable to proceed in a constructive and productive way. It is not saying "we are not going to talk about this", it is saying "we are not going to talk about this *now*." When you call a time out, both of you should agree that this is the best thing to do. I encourage you to talk about this before the need arises. Agree that, if one of you calls a time out, the other one must accept that the discussion is on hold. You could even decide beforehand how long a time out will generally last, though I suggest thirty minutes. You do not want to wait too long, just long enough for each of you to regroup.

Let me remind you that what really escalates an argument is the feeling of not being understood. If you just walk away while your spouse is yelling at you, they probably will keep doing it because they want you to understand their hurt and frustration. By calling a timeout for thirty minutes, you are sending the message that you want to resolve the problem after taking some time to calm down first.

Choose to love

Learning how to be angry and not sin is critical to the health of your relationship. Right after the Apostle Paul says "In your anger, do not sin", he also says "Do not give the devil a foothold" (Ephesians 4: 26-27 NIV). A foothold is a place from which one can launch an attack. The devil wants to control an area of your life, so he can use it to regularly attack you.

When you sweep things under the rug to avoid confronting your spouse when they offend you, it gives the devil a place to attack you from. The best way to avoid this is to not let the devil get that foothold. You do this by dealing with anger appropriately and by choosing to love.

Love does not dishonor

In 1 Corinthians 13, the famous love chapter, it says that love "does not dishonor others, it is not self-seeking, it is not easily angered, it keeps no record of wrongs" (1 Corinthians 13:5 NIV). God wants you to have this kind of love for your spouse.

In this verse, there are four characteristics of love. The first one is that love does not dishonor. One way to honor your spouse is to acknowledge and appreciate them for who they are and what they have done for you. Meanwhile, to dishonor is to criticize and berate your spouse by reminding them of their faults and weaknesses, which is easy to do when you are angry.

I have seen people do this to their spouse in front of others. However, listing their weaknesses and faults is not supportive of their growth or change. Instead, overlook those faults and speak words of appreciation to your husband or wife. Brag on them in front of others, let everyone know how proud you are of your spouse. This will certainly encourage them and build them up.

Love is not self-seeking

The second characteristic of love in this verse is that it is not self-seeking. To be self-seeking is to be selfish and focused on what you can get from another. At times in your marriage, you may find yourself acting selfishly; perhaps because there is a need in your life that is not being met or an issue that is continuing to bother you. To deal with this situation, you should lovingly talk to your spouse about how you are feeling. Do not allow selfishness to take over. Instead, choose to give and serve by putting your own needs aside for a time, and focus on the needs of your spouse.

Love is not easily angered

The third characteristic of love in this verse is that it is not easily angered. Being easily angered means displaying your displeasure over every little offense. However, when you choose to love, you choose to accept your spouse for who they are, defects and all. Of course they will do things that annoy you, so work on figuring out a mechanism to cope with them.

Life is full of people, including your husband or wife, who will act differently from you. Even if you cannot control that, you do have the power to choose how you will respond. Choosing to love means you overlook the little things and express your anger over the big things in ways that will lead to resolution and repair.

Love does not keep records

The fourth characteristic of love in this verse is that it does not keep a record of wrongs. When you say "You always" or "You never," you are simply reading the record of what your spouse has done before. When you avoid conflicts, instead of dealing with your anger in a healthy way, you write those things on your heart. This becomes your record of the offenses or wrongs against your spouse, just like a criminal record that the police would keep. Instead, talking about them, resolving your issues, allowing your spouse to apologize and releasing forgiveness, these steps really do have the power to erase that record.

Choose to forgive

Since we are talking about dealing with anger and resolving issues, we also need to talk about the power of forgiveness. Even if you do not want to, you will eventually hurt your spouse and they will hurt you as well. That hurt, of course, will make you angry. After you have expressed your anger, made a request and allowed your spouse to apologize, there is still one more thing you must do: forgive.

The Apostle Paul gives some instructions for us, regarding how to do that: "Get rid of all bitterness, rage and anger, brawling and slander, along with every form of malice. Be kind and compassionate to one another, forgiving each other, just as in Christ, God forgave you" (Ephesians 4:31-32 NIV). Paul contrasts two things here.

We are to get rid of all bitterness, rage and anger, brawling and slander, and every form of malice, as they come into our hearts when we do not deal with our anger appropriately. Bitterness can be the result of storing them inside and keeping a record of wrongs. Rage is the explosion of anger that happens when you reach the breaking point, caused by not dealing with an offense in an appropriate manner. Brawling is physical violence that is used to lash out, intimidate or get your way. Finally, slander is speaking about someone in such a way that they are cast in a bad light.

To the contrary, we are to be kind, compassionate and forgiving. Your response to hurt is a choice. You can either deny your anger and deal with it or choose to ignore it, and then live with the consequences of that. When you admit your struggle, own it or deal with it, you bring it into the light where you and your spouse can experience confession, repentance, compassion, forgiveness and, ultimately, healing. But it takes courage and commitment to love in this way. Fortunately, you are not alone.

Jesus is our example, the source of the courage we need to forgive. When he was on the cross, he forgave those who were brutally torturing him. "Jesus said, 'Father, forgive them, for they do not know what they are doing'" (Luke 23:34 NIV). Because of what he went through for us, we can now be forgiven. This is the basis for why we forgive others: we are to forgive because we have been forgiven. When you think about how much God has forgiven you, you are filled with an appreciation of God's grace and love. So, in the same way that he gave you grace and forgiveness, he enables you to extend grace and forgive others.

Forgiveness is both a decision and a process

Forgiveness is both a decision and a process. Depending on the depth of the hurt, it can either be something you can do quickly or it can take some time. In his book, *Forgiving the Unforgivable*, Dr. David Stoop has identified four steps that need to be done in order to forgive someone fully:

1. **Place blame appropriately**. Reflect on what happened and summarize what the other person did to hurt you. You may be tempted to blame yourself; however, even if you did play a part in whatever happened, this is about clarifying what happened to you.

2. **Grieve**. Allow yourself time to experience the emotional reaction of what happened. The two primary emotions of grief are anger and sadness, so it is okay to be mad for a while at the person who hurt you. You will also be sad when you realize what was taken away from you. Writing or talking about these feelings with a trusted friend or counselor are good ways to process your grief.

3. **Choose to forgive**. Even though forgiveness can be a process, at some point after grieving, you must let the person who hurt you off the hook. To do so, Dr. Stoop encourages us to use the following words. "Because through Jesus' death on the cross I have been forgiven, I am now unconditionally forgiving you for what you have done."

4. **Consider reconciliation and work to build trust again**. Reconciliation can only be done when both parties —the one hurt and the one who did the hurting— want

to reconnect. It is important to realize that, just because you forgive someone, you do not have to continue in a relationship with that person if you do not want to. For example, if that person is dangerous, either emotionally or physically, then reconciliation might not be the right thing to do. However, if they have repented and turned from their hurtful behavior, you can give them another chance if you want to. Remember that trust is something that develops over time. You need to forgive your spouse for driving drunk and crashing your car, but you do not have to give them the car keys until they have proven they will not do that again.[31]

Conclusion

Having a great marriage and a strong connection does not mean it will be pain or problem free. Conflicts will arise and you will hurt each other because you are both broken, sinful human beings who mess up. However, we all need a savior to change and heal us. We all need each other as well.

Your spouse is not your enemy, but your ally. They are a gift from God, sent to bless and strengthen you. Having a great connection that results in a great marriage is all about learning how to express your anger in a healthy manner, within an atmosphere of love and acceptance. As you learn how to resolve conflicts correctly, your connection with your spouse will turn up and become stronger rather than weaker. A long and enjoyable marriage will result when you learn how to use this skill and *"express your anger in a healthy way and give forgiveness generously"*.

With each other:

1. There are two extreme reactions to anger. The first one is to stuff it all inside and then explode; the second one is to react angrily to every little annoyance. Which one describes you and why?

2. Why do you think it is important to separate the issue from the person when you are angry?

3. Imagine you are angry at your spouse. Practice expressing your anger in a healthy way, by telling them about how you feel. Be sure to use "I" statements and make a simple request for something to change.

4. Talk about the four steps in the process of forgiveness: place blame appropriately, grieve, choose to forgive and consider reconciliation. Why is it important to go through this process and how does each step contribute to truly forgiving someone?

5. Is there someone you need to forgive? As you go through the process, be sure to ask God for his strength and support. Depending on whom you need to forgive, you can invite your spouse or a close friend to support you in this.

CHAPTER ELEVEN

SKILL #5

MANAGE YOUR MONEY

TOGETHER WITH WISDOM

We will manage our money together with wisdom

This is a book about how to turn up your connection in order to have a great marriage. To achieve this, we also need to talk about money.

There are a lot of good resources on managing your money, investing and budgeting that I encourage you to look into. My purpose here is to give you a few ideas on how to handle your finances in ways that will strengthen the connection you have with each other. Handling money can either be a blessing or a challenge in your marriage, and it does not matter what kind of job you have or how much you make.

I have heard that most couples argue over money and sex. However, in over thirty years of pastoral ministry, I rarely have a couple come to me with a sex problem. On the other hand, numerous couples have indeed come to me with money problems. Therefore, I encourage you to learn skill # 5: *"We will manage our money together with wisdom."*

Manage your money together

As a married couple, managing your finances starts with the commitment of doing it together. Remember that God's plan is that two people become one. Here is a practical way to live that out: all of your money, income, investments, debt and expenses become "ours." If your husband or wife brings debt into your marriage, that debt is now yours, and vice versa. In the same way, if you or your spouse earn a lot of money, that money belongs to both of you. Many wedding vows contain the phrase: "For better or worse, richer or poorer." This means that when you commit your lives to each other, you do so financially as well as emotionally.

Disclose everything

Uniting yourselves financially requires full disclosure. To start with, you should sit down and go over all your financial accounts together. Be sure to talk about ALL of your accounts, student loans, car loans, checking accounts, investments, savings and credit cards. Your spouse needs to know exactly what is going on financially in your life, both the good and bad. Have you had a bankruptcy or is your credit significantly damaged?

Do not hold anything back, tell each other everything. I have counseled many people who were surprised at the financial situation of their spouse. But you cannot keep it a secret: sooner or later, your husband or wife will find out about your financial history. It is always best to be up front about your finances before you get married.

Never hide anything

We have already talked about telling the truth and how important trust is to a marriage. If there is any area where this will be tested, it is in your finances. You might not be tempted to outright lie to your spouse, but you will be tempted to not always tell them everything. You may try to rationalize this by telling yourself: "I do not want them to worry." If you cannot pay your rent, it is better to talk about this than to have your spouse come home only to find that you received an eviction notice.

In the movies or on TV, you sometimes see someone setting up an account secretly to set money aside in order to buy a special gift for their spouse. This can be dangerous. It is not wise to have secrets when it comes to your marriage, especially financial ones. If God blesses you and you desire to surprise your spouse with a new car, may I suggest you give them a picture and talk it over before actually making the purchase.

Merge your accounts

The first step to managing your finances together is to set up a joint account or add each other to current accounts. Decide which one of you is going to be the primary manager. Revisit this from time to time to ensure that the needs of both you and your spouse are being addressed, as well as the bills getting paid on schedule and at a sufficient level.

When making financial decisions, do not be afraid to talk about all practical considerations. Do not make a financial decision or major purchases on your own: you are no longer free to think of it in terms of "my" money and "yours", now it is "our" money. This is important to establish at the beginning of your marriage, but also to continually remind yourselves of this as time goes by. If one of you pays the bills, it is crucial that the other person knows what is going on.

Identify your approach to money

You may find that you and your spouse have different attitudes when it comes to money. Some people are savers, while others are spenders.

Spenders are fun people to be around: they enjoy their money, can be generous, and make purchases spontaneously. Savers can be miserly, frugal to the point of depriving themselves of things they could easily afford to make their lives more comfortable. Before managing your finances together, first identify what is your attitude about money. Which one of these two styles seems more like you?

Nevertheless, neither of these two styles is healthy when taken to the extreme. The extreme spender may be carefree with their money and still be surprised when there is not enough to get to the end of the month. Meanwhile, the extreme savers may feel guilty if they use their money for anything other than necessities.

Managing your money wisely requires you to both save and spend. Savers need to learn how to let go of their money a little and not feel guilty about enjoying it. Spenders need to hold on to some of their money, for the future and for emergencies. Each of you has a perspective about financial matters, and neither of them is more correct than the other. In a marriage or relationship, it is wise to blend both of your approaches. Talk about how each of you used to manage your finances as individuals; then decide how you will blend each of your styles together.

Set goals

Once you have identified your financial styles, the next step is to talk about and then set some financial goals. What is important to you? What do you want your life to be like financially? Where do you want to be in the future? If you have a limited income and struggle every month to pay your bills, your goal might be to save for an emergency fund or to limit your spending so that you can pay all your necessary bills each month. Other goals might be to eliminate credit card debt, save for your child's college education, buy a house or save for retirement. The important thing is to plan and paint a picture in your minds of how you would prefer your life to be financially.

Track your spending

The only way to reach your financial goals is to set up a spending plan. However before you can create it, you need to see where you are currently spending your money.

The only way to do this is by tracking what you spend each month. Keep a log of what you spend each day, whether it is for gas in the car, a latte or a gym membership. At the end of the week, add up what you and your spouse have spent. Do this each week, so that at the end of the month you are able to see where your money is going.

The 10/10/80 spending plan

After you have identified your approach to money, set some goals, disclosed everything, merged your accounts, committed to managing your finances together and tracked your spending, the next step is to set up a spending plan or a budget. In some people's minds, budgets are bad because they sound limiting. For me, a spending plan sounds like fun —you can plan how you are going to spend your money each month!

Not only have Carrie and I learned about marriage from our Pastor, Dr. Jim Reeve, but he also has taught us the 10/10/80 plan.[32] If you want to be blessed, both financially and spiritually, I encourage you to follow it. Start by determining your monthly income, then take ten percent of that and give it to God. This act of obedience sets you up to see God supernaturally blessing you. Look at God's promise regarding finances:

> "Bring the whole tithe into the storehouse, that there may be food in my house. Test me in this," says the Lord Almighty, "and see if I will not throw open the floodgates of heaven and pour out so much blessing that there will not be room enough to store it" (Malachi 3:10 NIV).

A tithe is another word for a tenth or ten percent of your income. Carrie and I have been doing this consistently since we were first married, and God has certainly blessed us abundantly. Giving ten percent is an act of obedience and also a declaration of your trust in God to be your source.

10% to you – Emergency fund and savings

The next ten percent goes to you. Put aside ten percent of your income each month to turn it into savings and do your best to leave it there. A savings account functions as an emergency fund. What happens if your car breaks down? Or what do you do with an unexpected medical or dental bill? Once you have $1000 - $2000 set aside for emergencies, your next goal is to have the equivalent of three to six months of your take home salary, in case you or your spouse loses your job. After that, continue setting aside the ten percent, and start investing it for your retirement and saving to buy a house.

Solomon, again, shares his wisdom with us: "Go to the ant, O sluggard; consider her ways, and be wise. Without having any chief, officer, or ruler, she prepares her bread in summer and gathers her food in harvest" (Proverbs 6:6-8 NIV). Ants instinctively save for the future; they store up food in the summer, during harvest time, for the times when food will be scarce. The whole point of saving is to set aside a little every time you get paid, in order to allow that to grow.

Many people live paycheck to paycheck. Having an emergency fund could make all the difference when, not if, the hard times come. I know this is a challenging concept when you make just enough income to live, but something is always better than nothing. If you cannot do the full ten percent, then try to set aside the five percent or three percent, and do your best not to use it. It may also be helpful to set up two saving accounts: an emergency one that you can draw from when something unexpected happens and a general savings account that is allowed to grow.

Live on the remaining 80%

After paying your tithe and paying yourself, the remaining eighty percent is to cover your living expenses. Start out by writing down everything you have to spend money on each month: rent or mortgage payment, utilities, car insurance, gas, groceries, loan payments and other debt responsibilities. These items are called your fixed expenses. Then write out things that vary each month, such as eating out, buying clothes or going to the movies. Those items are discretionary items, those that you do not have to spend always; but that are there in case you need or want to. If you are paying God and paying yourself, go ahead and eat out with your spouse once in a while if you wish. The discretionary fund will enable you to enjoy your life with greater freedom, but will also prevent impulsive spending since it has a fixed limit.

Setting up and following a spending plan is the key to financial freedom. You can do this on paper or on your computer, although having it in writing is very important. You may be surprised at what you will learn about your financial situation. Many people think they have more money than they actually do. When you see the figures of your tithing, savings and fixed expenses written down, it may seem that what is left is not enough. Instead of cutting back on expenses, you will be tempted to cut back on your giving or saving.

If eighty percent of your income is not enough to live on, you and your spouse may have to explore some creative ways to stretch your spending plan by cutting back on expenses or coming up with ways to increase your income. To start with, decide which items on your spending plan are wants and which ones are needs. You need food, but you want cable TV. You need to pay your rent, but you want a new pair of shoes. Make sure to address the needs before the wants.

Once you have your spending plan in place and are tracking your spending, you can compare the two of them. The written plan is the ideal and the end of the month record is the real. You will be surprised at the results. I know this sounds like a lot of work, but it is worth it. Both you and your spouse will have to learn to say no to yourselves at times, in order to follow your spending plan. It is the only way to stay on target.

Spend less than you earn

The truth is that financial freedom comes when you spend less than you earn. Many people, unfortunately, do not live within their means. They spend more than they earn, by pulling from their savings each month or by using credit cards. If you do either of these things, you will struggle financially. If your income is not sufficient to tithe, save and pay all your expenses, then you need to evaluate your situation and make some changes. Either you need to increase your income or decrease your expenses. I realize this is easier said than done, but be honest and creative, and ask God to show you what adjustments can be made.

Avoid credit card debt

Credit card debt is a terrible trap. Why? Because the items you purchase with a credit card do not retain their original value, which makes it a bad debt. Do not be fooled by the minimum payment option on a credit card statement. If you just pay the minimum amount, it will take you a long time to pay off your balance.

Credit cards are convenient because they offer rewards and some say they are safer than a debit card, but you have to be disciplined about when and how you use them. Only use them if you track your spending and set aside the money for each purchase, so that you can pay the entire amount of the bill by the end of the month.

Use envelopes and pay cash

Many people, including us, find it helpful to put cash into various envelopes to keep track of what is spent each month.

One envelope is for groceries, another for clothes, another for eating out, etc; and the money you put in each is determined by your spending plan.

Whenever you use the money in an envelope, replace it with the receipt for your purchase; then, on the outside, write the date and the amount spent. When the money in a particular envelope is gone for the month, you have to stop spending in that category. If you find that you are short in one of the categories on a consistent basis, but have excess in another, make the appropriate adjustments.

Learn how to invest

As your income increases, you will find that you can start investing. When we first got married, Carrie had a good full-time job and I was only working part-time as a substitute teacher. We saved everything I had earned for a year and lived on just Carrie's income. We paid our tithe on our total earnings and limited our spending in order to save. A year later, I had a full-time job and we had saved enough for a down payment on a small house. That was one of the wisest things we ever did financially. While a house is a place to live, it is also an investment because it usually goes up in value over time. It was all possible because we remained disciplined during that first year of our marriage, saving enough for that down payment.

I encourage you to learn about investing, as well as how to manage your finances. One of the other things I did early on was to learn about mortgages, stocks, bonds and mutual funds. I am no expert, but when our financial advisor presents various options, I am glad that I know a little about what they are talking about.

Be a blessing

Not only does God want to bless you financially, he wants to use you to be a blessing. God's promise to Abraham applies to us today: "I will make you into a great nation, and I will bless you; I will make your name great, and you will be a blessing" (Genesis 12:2 NIV). Think of your finances as a river of blessing. God wants to pour finances and blessings into your lives for you to pour them into the lives of others. You cannot give what you do not have, so trust God to bless you and meet all your needs in abundance. Then you can give to others and be a channel of blessing for God to use.

Conclusion

Money can be both a blessing and a challenge. If you and your spouse lay a foundation of full disclosure, clear communication and following your spending plan together you will avoid many of the pitfalls that many fall into. When you agree together on how you will manage your money, you will find that, as partners, you can take care of each other in the best possible ways. If you want to turn it up, have a great marriage and a strong connection, it is critical to master this skill: *"We will manage our money together with wisdom."*

With each other:

1. Which financial style, spender or saver do you most identify with and why?

2. If you are not sure where you are spending your money each month, start tracking everything daily. Create a plan that you both will follow.

3. Identify what is currently missing in your financial situation and take steps to remedy it. Those things could be: merging your accounts, tithing, creating a spending plan, setting up an envelope system, learning about investing or giving to others.

4. Is there anything about your finances that you need to disclose to your spouse?

Turn it up!

PART FOUR
FINAL THOUGHTS

CHAPTER TWELVE

CONCLUSION

Turn it up is all about increasing the quality of your connection: great marriages and strong connections do not just happen by accident. If both you and your spouse are willing, then you can have a great marriage and the kind of connection that will be a great source of strength and joy. If you consistently monitor the quality of your connection and then do the things I have taught you in this book, you will turn it up and achieve what you really want —a great marriage that will last a lifetime.

Let me also say that there are no guarantees in life. You may do everything that I have talked about in this book, but things may not work out as you had planned or hoped. We live in a fallen world and we all make mistakes. Does that mean that you can give up and not even try to have a great marriage? No. You took that step of faith and got married. You gave your heart to another person and trusted him or her to love and care for you, just as they trusted you.

If you are not married and want to play it safe, then marriage may not be the right choice for you. If you want to have one of God's greatest blessings, then take that step of faith. If you want to have a life of love, choose to love, choose to be vulnerable, choose to trust, and then choose to be married to someone. Choosing to risk getting hurt, however, does not have to be a blind leap into the unknown. By reading and applying the principles in this book, you will be better prepared to handle the challenges that will inevitably arise in your relationship; and the better prepared you are, the more likely you will succeed. So take what I have shared with you and put it into practice. Knowledge that is not applied is useless, but knowledge that is used creates wisdom.

As you apply the lessons of this book, think about progress, not perfection. This is true especially with the skills we talked about. Do not forget that skills take time to learn and lots of practice to master. The more you use these skills, the more comfortable and better you will become at applying them when needed. Give yourself some grace and do not demand perfection. Also I suggest you give yourself the freedom to make mistakes. Make the commitments, use the skills and then look back to check all the progress towards your goal of having a great marriage and a strong connection.

Be sure to ask the connection question on a regular basis, "How's our connection?" and remember that connections are like a dimmer switch that gradually tends to diminish in strength and needs to be turned up. Making the five commitments and using the five skills on a regular basis will turn up the strength of your connection and increase its quality.

I never intended this book to be the final word on how to have a great marriage, but my goal is that it would be a practical guide that will equip you to have one. Hopefully, you have learned that great marriages do not just happen: they take effort, skill, investment of time and a determination not to quit. Your marriage will be what you make it and, with God's blessing and guidance, you too can have a great one.

Fairy tales end with the famous phrase "...and they lived happily ever after." This implies that the hero and his bride never had any problems after that. But we all know that real life is not like that. You will have challenges but, as I said before, your spouse is not your enemy —your spouse is your ally. As you face problems together, you will overcome and walk in the blessings of the Lord.

One last thought I want to share is that having a great marriage and strong connection is not just about you. Remember other people are watching. Those are your kids, friends, coworkers, extended family members and strangers who see you holding hands when you are going for a walk. Many of them, for example, are so hurt that they have given up on love or come to the conclusion that a good marriage is just for "lucky" people. Your kids and perhaps even your grandchildren are also wondering what love is all about, while looking at you and your relationship. You have an opportunity to give others proof that marriage is God's idea and that he will bless it when you do it his way. You can have a great marriage that becomes an example to others. At the end of your life, you will look back on a relationship that endured, flourished and was a source of blessing, not only to you but to many others as well. And as you give thanks to the Lord for his blessing, you will also realize that your marriage brought glory to God.

As I end this book, let me thank you for reading it. I hope you enjoyed it and found it helpful as well. I pray that God will bless you with a strong connection and a great marriage. I pray that he will guide you, fill you with his love and use you to be a blessing to others. I also pray the following words, which the Apostle Paul wrote to the church in Rome:

May the God who gives endurance and encouragement give you the same attitude of mind toward each other that Christ Jesus had, so that with one mind and one voice you may glorify the God and Father of our Lord Jesus Christ. (Romans 15:5-6 NIV)

ABOUT THE AUTHOR

Hi, I'm Kelly.

I'm a husband, Dad, Grandpa, Pastor, Police Chaplain, Marriage Coach but most importantly a follower of Jesus Christ. I have been married to my wife, Carrie for over thirty years and we've been blessed with a son, daughter, son in law and two grandkids. I love to be with my family, read, play golf, swim laps, ride my bike and take our dogs for their twice a day walks.

I am honored to be serving as one of the pastors at Faith Church in West Covina, where I have served for over thirty years. I also have the honor of serving as a Chaplain at the West Covina Police Department.

I'm passionate about helping couples turn their marriages around because I have personally felt the pain of a marriage in crisis. I have also seen firsthand the pain that comes to a family when there is a divorce. I'd rather be on top of the cliff helping people turn around than at the bottom with an ambulance taking them to the hospital.

My goal is to help married couples who are drifting apart reconnect so that they can have the marriage they really want. I do this by providing coaching to individuals and couples and teaching relationship tools in person and through books, videos, and articles. Please let me know how I can help you.

Thank you for buying my book. As a gift to you, I have a six (6) part video course entitled *5 things to stop drifting apart*. You can access it at https://turnitup.coach/freevideos.

For more marriage resources check out my website: https://turnitup.coach.

For individual and group premarital or marriage coaching and speaking requests, please contact me at kelly@turnitup.coach.

Follow me on social media at:

Facebook: https://turnitup.coach/facebook

YouTube: https://turnitup.coach/youtube

Twitter: https://turnitup.coach/twitter

LinkedIn: https://turnitup.coach/linkedin

ACKNOWLEDGMENTS

There are so many people who I want to thank for their support and input for this book. At the risk of skipping someone, here goes: Dr. Caroline E. DuPée, my loving wife who edited the first version of this book and made sure my writing made sense. Thank you for believing in me and this project so that my dream could become a reality. My kids Chris, Katie, son in law Andrew and grandkids whom I wrote this for so they could have successful marriages.

Dr. Jim Reeve for writing the forward and teaching Carrie and I how to be married. Pastor Bob Reeve who did our premarital counseling and is cheering us on from heaven. All the friends who wrote an endorsement for this book. Your words were so encouraging. Rick Koon for his concept of the three L's that every marriage needs. Diane Buers for her edits early on in this project and her continual encouragement. John Stanley for your input regarding the Beatles.

Albert Cuadra for giving the book a final edit and finding lots of things that needed fixing. Vladimir Lugo for making this possible. My friends Larry Franco and Danny Tienda who were there for me when my marriage was tested. The guys in my Tuesday Men's group: Albert, John S., John M, Eddie, Mack, Bill, Matt, Sean and David. You guys have been such a powerful source of strength for me.

Pastor Dan Reeve, the ministry staff and people of Faith Church. It is such a privilege to serve the Lord with you. Pastor Dawn Jackson who encouraged me to become a coach and led the way by becoming one herself. Pastor Stephan

Ichiriu for listening and praying for me and my family during a very difficult time.

Chief Richard Bell and all the active and retired members of the West Covina Police Department who have welcomed me into their family and taught me what courage, integrity, sacrifice and serving the Lord is all about. All the individuals and couples that have allowed me to coach them to have God's best in their lives and marriages. Finally, to my Lord and Savior Jesus Christ from whom all blessings flow. I pray you use this book for your glory and that it would help people come to know you.

NOTES

1. John Gottman, *The Seven Principles for making Marriage work* (Harmony Books, New York, 2015), 18.

2. Jeff and Jill Williams, *Marriage Coaching* (Springfield Ohio: Grace and Truth Relationship Education, 2011), 57.

3. Richard Koon conversation. He actually used the terms "Love, Like and Lust", but Diane Buers suggested that the word "lust" had too many negative connotations and that I change it to "longing". 20.

4. Henry Cloud and John Townsend, *Boundaries in Marriage* (Grand Rapids Michigan: Zondervan, 1999), 103.

5. Jim Reeve, s*ermon at Faith Church.*

6. "Trust." *Miriam Webster Dictionary* http://www.merriam-webster.com/dictionary/trust.

7. John and Julie Gottman, *The Man's Guide to Women (*New York, New York: Rodale, 2016), 58.

8. Cloud and Townsend, *Boundaries in Marriage*, 99.

9. https://www.freed4life.me/reasons-why-porn-is-bad/ destruction-testimonials/, retrieved 2013.

10. https://www.12step.org/the-12-steps/, retrieved on May 28, 2015.

11. James Reeve, *Sermon at Faith Church.*

12. Gary Chapman, *The Five Love Languages* (Chicago Illinois: Northfield Publishing 2010).

13. Dave Martin, *Sermon at Faith Church,* 2013.

14. Milan and Kay Yerkovich, *How We Love,* (Colorado Springs Colorado: Waterbrook Press, 2007), 11.

15. Mark Nickens, (2008). Search for God. Retrieved on April 2, 2015, from http://www.christiantimelines. com/God%20shaped%20hole.htm

16. Henry Cloud and John Townsend, *How People Grow* (Grand Rapids Michigan: Zondervan 2001), 284.

17. Bernard G. Guerney and Mary Ortwein, *Mastering the Mysteries of Love* (Frankfort Kentucky: Relationship Press 2008), 12.

18. Henry Cloud, *Integrity* (New York, New York: Harper Collins, 2006), 264.

19. Guerney and Ortwein, *Mastering the Mysteries of Love,* 6-9.

20. John Townsend, *Where is God* (Nashville Tennessee: Thomas Nelson, 2009), 5.

21. Cloud and Townsend, *How People Grow,* 265.

22. The concept of SMART goals is generally attributed to Peter Drucker and there are several versions. I adapted this acronym to make it relevant for making requests in a relationship. See Robert L. Bogue (2005) Use S.M.A.R.T. goals to launch Management by Objectives plan. *Tech Republic.com* Retrieved on May 21, 2015, from http://www.techrepublic.com/article/use-smart-goals-to-launch-management-by-objectives-plan/

23. Jim Reeve, *Sermon at Faith Church.*

24. Guerney and Ortwein, *Mastering the Mysteries of Love,* 14.

25. Jorge Castro and Lidia Soto, CSL Training at Faith Church .

26. Jorge Castro and Lidia Soto, CSL Training at Faith Church .

27. Steve Corbett and Brian Fikkert *When Helping Hurts* (Chicago Illinois: Moody Publishers 2009), 109.

28. Cloud and Townsend, *Boundaries in Marriage,* 136.

29. John Maxwell, Developing the Leaders Around You (Nashville Tennessee: Thomas Nelson 1995), 4.

30. Axelrod, J. (2006). The 5 Stages of Loss and Grief. Psych Central. Retrieved on March 25, 2015, from http://psychcentral.com/lib/the-5-stages-of-loss-and-grief/000617

31. David Stoop, Forgiving the Unforgivable (Ventura California: Regal Books 2005), 90-106.

32. Jim Reeve, Sermon at Faith Church.

APPENDIX A

Feeling Word List

Instructions – when you do not know how to describe how you are feeling, it may be because you are having a difficult time finding the right word. There are two sections to this list, pleasant or unpleasant. Go to the appropriate section then look over the words in all capitals to see which category best fits what you are feeling. Then look at the descriptive words in that category to best describe what is going on inside you. Once you identify the best words, be sure to tell someone you trust.

Source:

http://www.psychpage.com/learning/library/assess/feelings.html
retrieved on June 2, 2015.

Pleasant Feelings

OPEN	HAPPY	ALIVE	GOOD
Understanding	Great	Playful	Calm
Confident	Gay	courageous	Peaceful
Reliable	Joyous	Energetic	at ease
Easy	Lucky	Liberated	Comfortable
Amazed	Fortunate	Optimistic	Pleased
Free	Delighted	provocative	Encouraged
Sympathetic	Overjoyed	Impulsive	Clever
Interested	Gleeful	Free	Surprised

OPEN	HAPPY	ALIVE	GOOD
Satisfied	Thankful	Frisky	Content
Receptive	Important	Animated	Quiet
Accepting	Festive	Spirited	Certain
Kind	Ecstatic	Thrilled	Relaxed
	Satisfied	Wonderful	Serene
	Glad		free and easy
	Cheerful		Bright
	Sunny		Blessed
	Merry		Reassured
	Elated		
	Jubilant		

LOVE	INTERESTED	POSITIVE	STRONG
Loving	Concerned	Eager	Impulsive
considerate	Affected	Keen	Free
affectionate	Fascinated	Earnest	Sure
Sensitive	Intrigued	I\intent	Certain
Tender	Absorbed	Anxious	Rebellious
Devoted	Inquisitive	Inspired	Unique
Attracted	Nosy	determined	Dynamic
Passionate	Snoopy	Excited	Tenacious
Admiration	Engrossed	enthusiastic	Hardy
Warm	Curious	Bold	Secure
touched		Brave	
sympathy		Daring	
close		challenged	
loved		Optimistic	
comforted		re-enforced	
drawn toward		Confident	
		Hopeful	

Difficult/Unpleasant Feelings

ANGRY	DEPRESSED	CONFUSED	HELPLESS
Irritated	Lousy	Upset	Incapable
Enraged	Disappointed	Doubtful	Alone
Hostile	Discouraged	Uncertain	Paralyzed
Insulting	Ashamed	Indecisive	Fatigued
Sore	Powerless	Perplexed	Useless
Annoyed	Diminished	embarrassed	Inferior
Upset	Guilty	Hesitant	Vulnerable
Hateful	Dissatisfied	Shy	Empty
unpleasant	Miserable	Stupefied	Forced
Offensive	Detestable	disillusioned	Hesitant
Bitter	Repugnant	unbelieving	Despair
Aggressive	Despicable	Skeptical	Frustrated
Resentful	Disgusting	Distrustful	Distressed
Inflamed	Abominable	Misgiving	Woeful
Provoked	Terrible	Lost	Pathetic
Incensed	in despair	Unsure	Tragic
Infuriated	Sulky	Uneasy	in a stew
Cross	Bad	pessimistic	Dominated
worked up	a sense of loss	Tense	
Boiling			
Fuming			
Indignant			

Turn it up!

Difficult/Unpleasant Feelings

INDIFFERENT	AFRAID	HURT	SAD
Insensitive	Fearful	Crushed	Tearful
Dull	Terrified	Tormented	Sorrowful
nonchalant	Suspicious	Deprived	Pained
Neutral	Anxious	Pained	Grief
Reserved	Alarmed	Tortured	Anguish
Weary	Panic	Dejected	Desolate
Bored	Nervous	Rejected	Desperate
preoccupied	Scared	Injured	Pessimistic
Cold	Worried	Offended	Unhappy
disinterested	Frightened	Afflicted	Lonely
Lifeless	Timid	Aching	Grieved
	Shaky	Victimized	Mournful
	Restless	heartbroken	Dismayed
	Doubtful	Agonized	
	Threatened	Appalled	
	Cowardly	Humiliated	
	Quaking	Wronged	
	Menaced	Alienated	
	Wary		

APPENDIX B

Recommended Reading List

Beattie, Melody. *Codependent No More.* Halzenden Publishing 1992

Chapman, Gary. *The 5 Love Languages.* Northfield Publishing 2015

Cloud, Henry.

Changes that Heal. Zondervan 1993

9 Things you must Simply do to Succeed in Life and Love. Thomas Nelson 2007

Integrity. Harper Business 2009

Cloud, Henry and Townsend, John.

Boundaries. Thomas Nelson Publishing 1992

Boundaries in Marriage. Zondervan 2002

Boundaries with Kids. Zondervan 2001

How People Grow. Zondervan 2004

12 "Christian" Beliefs that can drive you crazy.

Zondervan 1995

Raising Great Kids. Zondervan 2000

Safe People. Zondervan 1996

Corbett, Steve, and Fikkert, Brian. *When Helping Hurts.* Moody Publishers 2009

Gottman, John.

The Seven Principles for Making Marriage Work. Harmony Books 2015

What Makes Love Last? Simon and Schuster 2012

The Man's Guide to Women. Rodale 2016

Scazzero, Peter. *Emotionally Healthy Spirituality.* Thomas Nelson 2006

Sorenson, Michael S. *I Hear You – the surprisingly simple skill behind extraordinary relationships.* Autumn Creek Press 2017

Stoop, David.

Forgiving the Unforgivable. Regal Books 2005

You are what you Think. Revell 2003

Townsend, John.

Boundaries with Teens. Zondervan 2006

Where is God? Thomas Nelson 2009

Hiding from Love. Zondervan 1996

Williams, Jeff and Jill. *Marriage Coaching – heart, hope and skills for a great relationship.* Grace and Truth Relationship Education, LLC. 2011

Yerkovich, Milan and Kay. *How we Love.* Water Brook Press 2008

Turn it up!

Portable
PUBLISHING GROUP

We are a creative publishing house focused on independent authors. We match the energy of the start up with the experience of a team of talents in all areas of editorial management. Our specialty is looking for inspiring authors, building unforgettable content and publishing books to be read around the world. We are more than a publisher: we are an agency for authors of the future.

@EditPortable

www.editorialportable.com
Contact: info@editorialportable.com

His book has been published in collaboration with **Tepui Media.**

Tepui Media is a company committed to strengthening the message of independent authors and amplifying their communicational impact. Tepui's working team is highly qualified in multimedia communications and includes many specialists in Digital Presence, Audiovisual Production, Content Strategy and Software Development.

For expert advice, contact

https://tepui.media

info@tepui.media

Made in the USA
Columbia, SC
23 November 2021

49625123R00128